AMBER

CHRONICLES FROM OBLIVION

Roberto, a middle class school teacher, finds himself regardlessly, involved in a paradoxical situation, at the limits of the imagination; two different eras merge in a mysterious way into a single amber-coloured reality. Lives that intersect, embrace, confront each other in what will be the main theme of this novel: the search for the occult direction of someone or something above all daring hypotheses. But, as is very often the case, the solution is closer than one might believe.

Chapter One

Tuscany, Italy.

Muffled noises. Meaningless words. It feels good here. I don't miss anything. I finally have time for me. In this endless space, my soul screams in silence, and my glazed eyes see without looking. Elaborate. Reconnect. Inside an unreal, delicate halo of amber light.

1065

He had been wandering the parched and thirsty countryside for days now; he had been longing for a small stream to get that damned dust off his throat and skin.
It had not rained for months, and the only people he had met since leaving the village were two bandits who had tried to rob him.
They had suddenly materialised in front of him, jumping out of a forest adjacent to the path, ordering him to stop and take out everything he had.
When they realised he was a poor man like them, one of them had tried to punch him in disappointment; but he was younger and had managed to escape through the woods.
For a while they had chased him, but then age got the better of them, and they had stopped to catch their breath, dividing it between swearing and cursing.

But then, rob him of what? He had nothing with him except a rusty old knife and an empty bag. The bread crusts had already been gone for a couple of days.

The sun was now behind the mountains, and Riccardo prepared to spend another night in the open air, torn between the constant fear of wolves and the hunger pangs that now gave him no respite.

Then he heard something, similar to the faint rustling that causes a light breeze through autumn leaves: but there was no wind, and it was full summer; therefore, it could only be the flow of a stream. As he got closer, the noise became more and more intense, and he was finally able to throw himself under a small waterfall of clear, refreshing water.

Riccardo was strong. His seventeen years spent almost entirely working the land had given him a tough physique; the painful beatings he had taken from his father had convinced him that he could endure anything except hunger, for which he was not prepared.

Good or bad, he had always found something to put under his teeth, although he had often been forced to pilfer for chickens, and bits of fruit, once he had been caught red-handed, with his sack full of apples, as he was walking away from his neighbour's field. He had had to work two days for free, to pay back those apples.

From then on, when he wanted to steal something, he went far away, where people did not know him. But even this system was not safe: it could happen that he would be away for days without being able to find even one chicken.

But this time it would be different. He had not left his home for a few days, but for good. He would never go back to that filthy village, where the high point of life was a quickie with Camilla, a young woman whom everyone described as ugly as starvation, but whom they then frequented without any restraint; they knew that she also granted her favours for a fee, but most of the time the reward was a bit of bread or a couple of pigeons.

And then he was fed up. Enough of that life! For a long time Riccardo had wanted to escape, to go away, to seek other paths, in the belief that the world was not just the dreary country where he had been born; he did not want to end up like his father, that filthy being who thought almost exclusively of getting drunk and beating everyone around him, including him and his mother.

She was dead, his mother. He had found her, huddled on the stone in front of the fireplace, her head smashed in; his father had said she had fallen, but Riccardo had never believed it. Three years earlier, his little brother, just four years old, had fallen and died too. That's enough.

Early the next morning he set off, with a great desire in his head: to see the sea.

Riccardo, despite his first impression, was a fairly well-read young man for the environment and times in which he lived. His good fortune had been to meet Edoardo, an addict traveller who had visited many important cities.

Edoardo was a native of his own village, and had learned to read and write Latin while working in Pisa at a solicitor's office, first as a servant, then as a secretary. He had made quite a name for himself in that city, and had even started a family, a beautiful family indeed, with four children, three of them boys. Then one day he had wanted to return to see the village where he had been born, and had brought his loved ones along to show them the places of his youth.

While they were crossing the Pisa mountains, they had been attacked by bandits, who abounded in those days. The bandits had killed his children, raped and murdered the two women, tortured and severely wounded Edoardo to the point of believing him dead. Then they started drinking, near the still-warm corpses, and left shouting and laughing drunk on wine and beer.

Edoardo was not dead: but it was as if he were. He prayed for three whole days that he would die, weeping and despairing over the fate of his loved ones, unable to move because of a bad leg wound.

He was found in agony by a merchant passing by in his cart, escorted by four soldiers, who gave him first aid and had the bodies buried. Edoardo asked and obtained to be left near his village, and dragged himself to the first houses.

Riccardo, who was then eleven years old, saw him at the edge of the village dragging himself painfully and helped him to his old, deserted and half destroyed house. After a week, Edoardo realised he would never walk again, and became completely dependent on Riccardo, who for his part did his utmost to help him, perhaps identifying him with the figure of the father who had never been a real father.

The two quickly became great friends, and Edoardo taught the boy many things in the next five years.

Riccardo tried in every way to keep the man's spirits up: he told him everything that happened in the village and even built him a kind of perforated chair under which a bucket could be slipped, which served very well for bodily needs.

One winter morning he found him dead, sitting on the chair he had built, with a smile on his lips that would become his most recurrent dream.

He had cut his hand with an axe, and had let the blood drain from his body until his heart had stopped beating.

Riccardo liked to talk about the sea with the friar who came to his village every three or four months to beg for the convent; Friar Candido also liked to stop for a chat, if only to rest a little, and Riccardo peppered him with questions about how life was outside his village. So he had heard about the sea, and of all the things he had never seen it was the one that fascinated him most of all; that mass of water whose end could never be seen was an irresistible attraction for someone like him, used to limited spaces: there was the hen house, then came the house, then the forest and the mountains. For almost all the villagers, the world ended there.

A distant howl woke him from his thoughts; it would soon be dark, and if he did not quickly find a suitable tree to spend the night in, there would be serious trouble.

He saw it at the last moment. The driver of the Mercedes also saw it, but not fast enough to avoid the impact. The blow was tremendous, and Roberto flew off his bicycle and crashed into a large plane tree.

He woke up in a dimly lit room and looked around painfully, but the dim amber light illuminated a completely empty room.

Only then did he realise that a tube was attached to his wrist, and that a headache like this had not been felt for years. He thought back to what had happened, but the only memory he had was the front of a Mercedes and a frightened face in the passenger seat; he couldn't even tell if it was that of a man or a woman.

The light in the room suddenly came on, forcing Roberto to close his eyes; when he opened them again, he saw a young woman in a white coat pulling a trolley full of medicines.

"What time is it?"

"Ah, he's awake!" Said the woman in a slight southern accent, "It's twenty past six... in the morning."

He had not paid attention before, but now, looking in the direction of the window, Roberto realised that it was dark.

"What happened to me?"

"I don't know exactly... all I know is that you had a bad accident... and it's a good thing you had your helmet on!"

"No, I meant... what did I do to myself?" asked Roberto again, moving his head slowly.

"Look, don't get excited now... surely nothing serious, otherwise you wouldn't be talking to me..." The nurse stifled a giggle that seemed really out of place to Roberto, then leaned towards him, casually showing off a generous cleavage framing the top of a very ample bosom.

"I should warn someone."

"Already done, rest assured! In your wallet we found his identity card, and we phoned the registry office. They gave us your wife's address and we got in touch with her... she should be here in the morning. Time to arrive from Florence. Now get some more rest, at seven o'clock the ward doctor arrives and you can talk to him."

My wife! Roberto thought as the nurse switched off the light and closed the door. *My wife! That nasty piece of work! I don't want my wife to come here!*

Two years earlier they had split up, after living together for three years without children, without emotion, without love. They had only married because Anna was pregnant; then the miscarriage at four months, and the certainty that nothing would ever go smoothly between them again.

It had been a decision made by mutual agreement, without trauma, and she had gone to live in Florence, where she worked at a newspaper. She told herself that she was a journalist at a national newspaper, but in reality she spent all day and many nights editing the articles written by others. She had found another man, a certain Casciani, a divorced man with three daughters, a civil servant whose greatest aspiration was to have his salary credited to the bank so that he could pay alimony to his ex-wife who was pestering him with constant requests for money.

And now she was about to arrive, to remind him of five years of useless life....

A sudden terror assailed him. *But what have I really done to myself? What if I can no longer walk? What if I can no longer get out of this bed?*

He tried to move his legs slightly. It was as if someone had stabbed him in the back, but a sigh of relief came out when he realised that his legs were responding to his calls. In spite of the great headache that was tormenting him, he sank into a sleep full of sun, heat, sea, and he was Superman, and he was running on the water so fast that his legs could hardly be seen.

1065

"What are you doing up that tree?"
Riccardo jolted awake, in danger of falling. It was dawning, and the light was still poor.
"I spent the night here, but I'm leaving right now, excuse me," he said, looking at the young woman who was looking at him with an amused air.
"Apologise? What for? It's not like that tree is mine! You can stay there all day for me. I just can't understand why you didn't go all the way to the village... someone would surely have taken you in."
Riccardo followed the girl's outstretched arm with his eyes, and saw a few houses peeping out of the light morning mist that heralded another sultry day. If he had walked another thirty steps the night before, he would have bumped into them.
"Who are you?"
"Riccardo. My name is Riccardo." he said, stepping down from the tree with an awkward leap, to say the least, that made him fall ruinously at the woman's feet. He immediately got up again, with an indifferent air, while the young woman barely held back her laughter.
Only then did he notice the strange colour of those eyes that continued to stare at him in curiosity: they were as green as spring grass wet with morning dew. She must have been about fifteen years old, and her hair pitch black. But such eyes Riccardo had never seen.
"You live in that village?"
"Yes. My name is Celeste, and I am the blacksmith's daughter."
"Perhaps you can help me... I am going to Liburna, a village by the sea. I've been walking for nine days

now, and I haven't found anyone to ask for directions... can you show me the way?"
"No... I know it's not very far, but I've never been there. If you follow me I'll take you to my father's...he knows where it is, because he goes there two or three times a year, because of certain jobs to be fixed and to buy stuff; next time he promised to take me with him. Are you hungry?"
It had been three days since Riccardo had eaten anything but roots, but his pride prevented him from getting too unbalanced.
"No, hungry no, but if you had some fruit I would take it for the journey...of course I could do some work to repay you for your trouble."
"You're lucky. Yesterday morning my mother and I made bread. Follow me."
Celeste set off towards the village, and Riccardo followed her, trying not to think about all that waddling movement of the hips in front of him.

The lane leading to the houses was narrow and full of holes; it was probably only the lane connecting to the fields, while the main entrance to the village was in the opposite direction. Riccardo had walked alongside the woman, but since she was walking in the middle of the road, she had difficulty keeping her balance, having to avoid the many stones and bushes that obstructed her path.
Arriving in front of the house, Celeste entered, and motioned for Riccardo to follow her.
The room was very large, as it also served as a workshop; in front of the large lit fireplace was the blacksmith, busy fixing a wooden handle to a knife; further on two benches and a large solid looking table occupied the centre of the room.

Sitting at that table was a woman, probably Celeste's mother, who was peeling onions; to Riccardo they seemed enormous, and made his mouth water.

"There, that's my father, the blacksmith; his name s Raterio," Celeste said to Riccardo. Then she walked over to where the man was working. "Father, this s Riccardo; he is from another village, and he is lost... he wants to know the direction to go to Liburna."

The man's eyes settled on the guest, then a deep voice said, "Of course. It is not very far... from here it is two days' walk."

Two days. Just two days. Riccardo felt like embracing the man.

"Today," Celeste resumed, "you can stay and eat something with us. We have my mother's famous onion soup. It's delicious, especially with the bread we made yesterday. And then we also have cheese and some wine."

"Thank you, but I wouldn't want to inconvenience you too much..." Said Riccardo, hoping for a little insistence, which did not take long to arrive.

"No bother at all," the young woman reassured him, "Where three people eat, four people eat. While we wait, you can come with me and help me to pick the apples. Come."

She moved outside, motioning for him to follow her.

1998

Roberto was swimming offshore in a warm, flat sea when he felt a stabbing pain in his left arm; terror invaded him, fearing he had been attacked by a shark.

He awoke with a groan, and saw the nurse from earlier who was fiddling with the IV needle planted on the back of his arm where he had felt the pain. She was so bent over him that this time he could also see the continuation of the earlier spectacle.

"So? How are we this morning?"

Standing in the middle of the room was a man in a white coat who was reading a paper contained in a blue folder; he was blond, with a childlike face that betrayed his young age, despite an unkempt beard that hid his chin.

"Do you remember your name?"

"Roberto. Roberto Altomiri."

"Do you realised that you had a bad accident? Anyway, we took X-rays, and there are no fractures. You hit your head...Imagine that it took us twenty minutes to remove your leather helmet. Nurse, are you finished with that IV?"

"Yes, doctor...do you need anything else?"

"No, let's go ahead. You try not to move. At ten o'clock we'll give you a CT scan, and if all goes well in a couple of days we'll send you home."

"Thank you." whispered Roberto as the two left the room. He turned his head to the right side, and only then did he realise that behind the screen dividing the room was another bed. From the position he was in, he could only see the backboard; therefore, he had no way of knowing if the bed was occupied. He tried listening, trying to hear a breath, a cough, the

sound of movement: nothing. Evidently, the next bed was empty. *Fine...it means I don't need to talk to anyone. At least until my wife arrives. Then she'll do all the talking. Then we'll be back to square one.*
His head was still aching, but surely that was normal after such an accident.
He tried once more to remember how the events had unfolded... but... Damn! The accident had happened at nine o'clock in the morning, he had no doubt because he was on his way to work... and if it was now seven o'clock in the morning, that meant he had slept almost twenty-four hours! Damn! A whole day! Good thing the school holidays had already started and the children would not miss him.

Roberto Altomiri was a primary school teacher, one of those who liked to call himself old-fashioned, even though he was only thirty-six years old. Teaching was his reason for living, and he boasted that he had never missed a class in twelve years. Sometimes he had gone to work with a high fever, once he had even broken his arm getting off the bus right in front of the house. But the next morning he was there, in the classroom, with his good plaster supported by a scarf, talking about mathematics; indeed, he had allowed his boys to write their names on the white surface of the plaster. Someone had even soiled his shirt cuff with coloured markers. Never mind.
He loved his children to the point of secretly weeping when they finished primary school, and he tried to prepare them well, knowing that with a good basis they would be better able to face the life ahead of them.
On the morning of the accident he was supposed to have a refresher course together with other teachers;

it was a study on music used as a vehicle of knowledge of the outside world, and Roberto absolutely did not want to miss it.

His thoughts were interrupted by light, a very strong amber coloured light coming from somewhere in the room; and in that light was a tree, and above the tree a young girl dressed in a kind of monk's habit, laughing, picking apples and throwing them towards him. And then she was laughing again. It went on for a couple of minutes that seemed an eternity to Roberto, then the light went out and the vision, as it had come, disappeared.
My God, what is happening to me?

1065

"Stop, please! I don't know where to put them anymore!"

"Lay them on the grass. Later I will put them in my lap. Can't you see what a long dress I have? Do you know how many apples fit in here?"

Celeste laughed, and continued picking apples and throwing them with precision towards Riccardo, who quickly deposited them on the ground, finding it all very amusing: but he hoped with all his heart that the fun could continue in another way.

"Now stop it," said Riccardo, "Don't pick any more, otherwise we won't even carry these apples in a barrow."

"All right. Help me down. I can't do it alone."

"Come on, jump," said Riccardo, bringing himself under the tree and stretching out his arms, "I'll catch you!"

"What if you don't catch me? I don't want to end up on the ground."

"Can't you see I'm right under you? How can you escape me?"

He barely had time to finish the sentence when Celeste launched herself, ending up exactly in the man's arms; but the weight made them both fall, and as they rotated they found themselves with their mouths a palm's width apart; they stood still, looking into each other's eyes, anticipating beforehand and with growing excitement an inevitable kiss that was delayed in coming.

But then it was an explosion of sensuality. The two entwined bodies rolled in the grass, until the woman stood up, and holding out her hand to Riccardo said 'Come. Here I am afraid someone might see us.

Let's go somewhere safer." They ran towards the woods, making an incredible number of small green locusts jump away hidden in the grass; then they slipped under the trees, and after walking a good distance through the woods, they stopped panting in the shade of a large oak tree.
On a low branch of that tree a squirrel peeped out; he seemed ready to enjoy the scene, but then he decided he didn't care, and with a leap he jumped to the ground and left.

It felt good there, sheltered from the heat of that blazing June; Riccardo and Celeste made love impetuously, heedless of the fact that they had only met two hours before, both discovering a happiness they had never dreamed could exist.

"Holy Mother of God! What happened to you?" At the very moment that Roberto's wife entered the room with an air of surprise and anguish (but that was her speciality) he had the sensation of being prey to a frightening and inappropriate erection. He quickly looked under the sheet, just to be sure, and what he saw could only confirm the fact. Not that she wasn't still desirable, indeed; but he had just recovered from the appearance of that strange woman throwing apples at him, and now this. Just as his wife walked in. *Am I crazy? What's happening to me?*

'They found me last night at the newspaper office...I don't even know how they knew I was there. They told me you'd had a terrible accident, and I immediately rushed over. What did you do to yourself?"

Rushed. She said she rushed! From Florence to here is at most a two-hour drive! Marta certainly would have rushed!

"I seem to have done well. I shouldn't have any bones broken...just a few bruises here and there...but I hit my head. Luckily, I was wearing a helmet."

"But how did it happen?"

"A Mercedes ran into me...I only remember that it was white..."

"You and your ecological manias! But couldn't you have got a driving licence like everyone else? No, you have to go around with your bicycle, that ridiculous striped helmet and the white mask in front of your mouth! I told you something would happen to you sooner or later...never once do you listen to me! If I had been with the car..."

Shut up! Did you come to check on me or to break my balls?

The car thing was an old story. Roberto had never wanted to get a driving licence. He said it was useless in a world full of transport. Besides, cars pollute, they stink, they are dangerous and they kill a lot of people on the roads and in Arab countries.
He had never liked cars, even though he understood very well that for many people it was indispensable to have one; and then car factories employed a lot of people. But he believed that no one had ever seriously and constructively addressed the search for a clean and viable alternative to oil.
His was a life choice. He had even joined a club of hardened ecologists, and on Sundays they all went on long bike rides in a group. They were good together. They were Sunday friends, the kind you never see during the week; and it was on one of those famous Sunday excursions that he had met Marta. They liked each other right away and got together, even though they had both agreed to maintain their independence: he had a serious relationship breakdown behind him and she had a very sad one.
They met two or three times a week, usually at Roberto's house, and there they talked about everything: politics, religion, ecology... but they had not yet made love. Their shyness blocked them, and Roberto often wondered which one of them would take the first step, and...and in the meantime the erection showed no signs of abating. In fact, Roberto was beginning to feel an intense heat, as if... Oh, my God! There he was, with his wife in front of him, babbling like an old maid, and he...and he...even a

moan of pleasure escaped him, and he turned his face towards the pillow to stifle it.

"What's the matter? What's the matter? Do you feel sick? Did they X-ray you?" the woman's shrill, slightly altered voice shook him, pulling him out of that awkward state.

He thought of him and his wife the rare times they had made love: a pitiful thing.

All without enthusiasm, without participation... yes, maybe the first two or three times. But then the monotony had taken over the emotions.

Now they had reached the point of unbearability. It was mutual, and they both knew it very well. Those rare times when they met, they put on a good face, trying to act nice; but in the long run, this attitude had a grotesque quality.

"Huh?!? Ah, yes...I've already told you that I have nothing broken...in the morning they do my CT scan, and if it's negative they send me home."

"Just as well...do you need anything? Pyjamas, a pair of slippers..."

'No no, I don't need anything...' lied Riccardo. Pyjamas were the least of his thoughts, although perhaps they would have come in handy now. But the mere thought that he owed his wife gratitude made him sick. He actually needed several little things, but he would ask Marta for them as soon as he was able to phone her.

Marta! But why aren't you here instead of this woman now?

"Then I'll go."

That's it, go.

"Today I have to do a report on an important congress at the Palazzo Pitti...you know, they're talking about the painters of the Italian seventeenth century, and they've given me the job of interviewing the professors and critics. Apparently, Vittorio Sgarbi is also there."

Give me a break! Imagine if they entrust such an important service to someone who has the same artistic sense as a monk seal... you interviewing Sgarbi! But who are you kidding? At most you'll be there taking notes while a real journalist asks the questions...

'Bye. I'll call you in a couple of days. Get well soon."

Get well soon. Like you care. But go to hell, and think about keeping your civil servant warm!

Roberto looked up, to say goodbye, and what he saw left him stunned. The one standing in front of him, the one looking at him with eyes as green as two emeralds, was not his wife. It was the girl in the monk's habit. And she was smiling at him, as if she was the cause of his latest misadventure under the sheets.

By now there is no longer any doubt. I'm really going crazy.

1065

The onion soup was delicious. Riccardo was hungry like a wolf, but he forced himself to eat in a cold and detached manner, while he felt Celeste's eyes on him that wouldn't leave him for a moment.
"Why are you heading for the sea?" asked Raterio without taking his eyes off his bowl of soup.
It was a question he dreaded. He did not know what to answer. In fact, even he did not know the precise reason for that journey... indeed, he did know: he wanted to leave home, to live in another place, to meet new people, to have other opportunities. The world must have been so big! He decided to be honest.
"I have never seen it. And there is a friar, Candido, who sometimes passes through our village and tells me about the sea."
"Candido? He also often comes by here... he is always looking for something to take to the convent." said the blacksmith's wife, "The last time he came by was a couple of months ago."
"Would you like a piece of cheese?" asked Celeste, seeing that the guest's bowl was empty.
"Thank you, but just a small piece, just to taste," replied Riccardo carelessly, trying not to let himself realise that he would devour the whole wheel, including the rind.
"In three days I have to go to Liburna to buy a tool" resumed the blacksmith, "If you can wait we will make the trip together. Celeste will also come... she too has never seen the sea. Unfortunately, we have only one daughter, so my wife will have to stay at home to look after the chickens and the fields. We

won't be gone more than five or six days in all anyway."

To Riccardo that proposal seemed the most beautiful thing in the world.

The blacksmith's family consisted of three single people, which was quite unusual at that time, but after their first daughter his wife had never been pregnant again. They owned the house where they lived, and worked several fields cultivated with cereals and onions. They also owned about thirty hens and a donkey, which was regularly loaded with firewood. For the hens, Raterio had built a hen house that looked like a real fortress; it had become necessary after foxes had devoured all his beasts a few years earlier.

'You'll be able to sleep in this room... luckily it's warm, and a bit of straw in that corner will suffice,' said Celeste's mother.

That's what was missing! The bedding for the night! But where were they? It was the first time that Riccardo had seen a house without the necessities for sleeping.

"But where do you spend the night?" he asked. A crystalline laugh came out of Celeste's mouth.

"My father divided the room. We sleep behind that wall. We have comfortable beds and bed pots at hand."

"And when it's cold? How do you get warm if the fireplace is in this room?" urged Riccardo.

"We have another one where we sleep...we need lots of firewood, but luckily that is never lacking...just go to the woods behind the house. And then we have the donkey to carry it up here," replied Celeste's mother.

Damn! Two fireplaces...a room used only at night...and a donkey! They must have been a rich family. It seemed a nice thing to him, although he couldn't see the point of it. There was only one room in their house, and they didn't even have bed pots for the night.

"Alright, I'll leave with you...anyway, a day or two makes no difference to me. But in the meantime I want to help you with something to do, to repay you for your hospitality."

"Don't worry," said Raterio pleasantly surprised by that answer, "I have to repair the roof of the house, which is now beginning to be old. This is the right season, and I want to do it before it starts raining. You will help me. It will only take two or at most three days. Finish eating the cheese and then take this knife: outside, behind the house, you will find some stacked poles. Start removing their bark. I will join you immediately."

Riccardo got up immediately, happy to be of use; he took the piece of cheese, and brandishing the knife like a sword, he started towards the door.

The poles were stacked at the back of the house; Riccardo immediately noticed that most of them were short and of similar size, while one was a real tree: long and at least four times as big as one of the other poles. Evidently that one would be used as the central support point, while the others would form the sides of the roof, where the branches, thatch and then the stone shingles would be placed, providing the inhabitants of the house with good shelter from the scorching summer sun and the freezing winter rains.

He picked up the highest pole of the pile and began to bark it vigorously: the knife was sharp and ran across the surface of the wood evenly, allowing him to peel off long pieces of bark from the trunk that fell silently at his feet.
Under that blinding sun, he began to sweat profusely, until a few salty drops entered his eyes and forced him to raise his head to wipe his forehead with the back of his arm.

1998

He was sweating. It seemed as if his pores were rejoicing at spurting out all those drops of salt water. By now the sheet had changed colour, and had become a veritable puddle in which Roberto splashed like a frog. He firmly grasped the cord hanging from the head of the bed and pulled hard. Through the top glass of the door he saw a red light flashing in the corridor.

He had had a CT scan, and when he had returned to his room he had found his bed made up with clean sheets. Although the nurses (strange, until now he had only seen female faces, apart from the ward doctor) had noticed his misadventure during his wife's visit, no one had opened their mouths. After a long tug of war he had managed to get a portable phone and had called Marta.
And then he had found a cup of broth on the bedside table. Someone must have brought it, although he hadn't seen anyone. Hot broth, with such an intense taste and smell of onions that it made his eyes water; but he had managed to drink it all, and now he wanted to take a nap. But he was sweating. Damn, how he was sweating!
I must have horse fever. Let's hope someone will come.
The door swung open and the woman in the friar's habit entered.
Roberto lost consciousness.

When he woke up, he found himself in front of a nurse he had never seen before.

He was extremely tired, as if he had unloaded a whole truckload of bricks by himself. He was no longer sweating, and they had changed the bed again. They had moved it twice without him noticing. Then he saw the doctor from before; he was by the window, looking out.

"More tests will have to be done," he said, "I don't like this story. I have never seen such sweating without a line of fever. We'd better call a dermatologist."

"Doctor..." whispered Roberto.

"Ah, he's awake!" replied the doctor, turning and leading the way to the bed, "I really wanted to talk to you. Have you had or have any illnesses that we should be aware of?"

"No. I suffered from colitis three or four years ago, but apart from that I haven't had anything else."

"It's a very strange thing...he was sweating so much...and the strangest thing is that we tested his fever. Thirty-six point eight. So a very normal temperature. How do you explain that?"

I have to explain it? But aren't you the experts? We pay top money for healthcare to work properly and then we have to diagnose ourselves?

' I can't explain it. I mean, I really don't know. It's the first time it's happened to me,' Roberto replied, shoving the sentence he had been thinking back down his throat.

"So," the doctor continued, "we should relate this phenomenon to the accident you were in."

Well done. You are such a genius.

"I'll have more tests done on you. And I'll send you a dermatologist."

I know what I need. I'd need a platoon of psychiatrists. Forget the dermatologist.

As soon as the doctor and the nurse had left, Roberto took his courage in both hands and tried to take stock of the situation. He did not feel calm: he was alone, at the mercy of his crazy visions; but he pulled himself together and tried to think.
Until then, he had accepted everything passively, so he decided that from now on he would tackle the situation head-on. He did not know precisely how, but he would do it.
He was sure it was a trick of his mind, and he was equally sure it was a consequence of the big blow to the head. But those visions seemed so real, so real... it was hard to distinguish reality from fantasy.
He had seen that strange woman three times: once she had thrown apples at him, another time she had taken the form of his wife, the last one (or at least he hoped it was the last one, but in his heart he had a feeling he would see her again) she had entered his room as if she were a nurse.
He had had that embarrassing adventure with his wife there, and ten minutes earlier he was sweating like a horse after running the grand prix.
Quite a balance, no doubt about it.
A sudden noise from behind the screen forced him to turn in that direction. The sound was slow, monotonous, as if someone was planing a wooden plank.
From his position he could not see what the noise was caused by, so with great effort he got up and sat down on the bed. He turned around, grabbed the movable perch that held the IV bottle and moved it towards the end of the bed, taking care not to dislodge the tube from the needle.

He let himself fall forward, finding his head brushing against the backboard. He then turned his face towards the bed behind the screen.

Sitting on the floor with his back against the bed was a man; with one hand he held a wooden pole firmly in place, while with the other he removed its bark using a large knife with a pointed blade. The man wore a short robe, and his legs were hairy like a bear. As Roberto was getting the irresistible urge to pick up a pole too and start debarking it, the man looked up and looked at him intensely; then he whispered, smugly, "Riccardo..."
"But what is going on in this hospital?" cried Roberto in a panic.
His words fell on deaf ears. An amber cloud suddenly appeared, hiding everything between the screen and the wall. Then, just as it had appeared, the cloud disappeared, and Roberto realised that this last nightmare had gone with it.
Exhausted by fatigue and emotion, he fell asleep.
And he dreamed of the sea again.

1065

"The sea is over there, beyond those trees," said Raterio.
The sea! Riccardo couldn't stand it any longer. He wanted to see it, touch it, smell it; he quickened his pace, aware that now only a few steps separated him from the object of his desires.
They had walked two days, stopping several times to let Celeste rest, and finally on the morning of the third day they had arrived.
"Easy!" exclaimed Celeste, laughing, "we can't keep up with you... slow down! Wait for us!"

Raterio smiled smugly. He was beginning to get used to the young man's enthusiasm, and he had to admit that he was a good worker, quick and precise; in the previous days, during the repair of the roof, he had had the opportunity to appreciate his remarkable ability to adapt to a wide variety of situations.
He had learnt how to saw wood to form joints; he knew how to hammer in nails and use hemp and willows for bindings. He was as agile as a cat, and when he climbed on the roof he immediately assessed which poles were at risk and avoided climbing on them.
Raterio concluded that without that young man's help it would have been impossible for him to finish the job in such a short time. He would not have minded if Riccardo and Celeste... after all, he had no sons, and someone had to continue blacksmithing.

They walked through a resin-scented pine forest and stood on top of a huge boulder jutting out onto the beach below.

Riccardo looked towards the horizon, and thought he had never seen anything so beautiful.
The expanse of water ended there, and merged with the blue of the sky into a single colour; a light morning breeze rippled the surface of the sea, making it look like a living, throbbing thing.

Riccardo had often wondered what lay beyond the sea. Edoardo had told him that theologians and scientists thought the earth was a flat disc stopped in the sky, and that the sun, moon and stars revolved around it. Many times Riccardo had lain down in the cornfields to scan the sky on clear summer nights, and watching the stars all move in the same direction, he had been assailed by the doubt that perhaps it was the earth that revolved... but he had never told anyone, lest he be taken for a fool. What did he know about it? He was neither a theologian nor a scientist. One thing, however, he could not understand: if the earth was flat, where did the sea go? Could it be that that great mass of water was all enclosed between the mountains? It had to be, otherwise it would have fallen from the earth...but fallen where? What was under the earth? Perhaps the good Lord had built an underground pipe through which the water passed and returned to the other side....

"Look at those big birds!" exclaimed Celeste, pointing to a myriad of seagulls strolling peacefully on the beach below.
"I often see them when I come to the sea... they look like crows, only they're white and a bit bigger."
"And they have different beaks," said Riccardo.
"So they don't look like crows!" said Celeste amused.

They walked down a steep slope, taking great care not to slip and clinging to some roots sticking out of the ground; when they reached the beach Riccardo noticed with amazement that he was not walking on earth, but on fine sand on which it was difficult to walk.

For a moment he was afraid of sinking, but the confidence with which Raterio was advancing calmed him down, and he walked the last few metres that separated him from the water, surprising himself with the warmth of the sand that entered his leather sandals with every step.

He touched the water, and it was a wonderful feeling. He was thirsty, but he knew it was not possible to drink; during the journey Raterio had explained to him that seawater was not good for that purpose, and that even to wash one's face one had to be careful, because it made one's eyes sting; Riccardo knew all this, but he had pretended not to and had thanked him for the advice.

"Now let's go to the village. It's not very far - it's over there, in that direction. You can see the houses. It is much bigger than our villages. A lot of people come here, mostly traders and travellers. We walk along the beach; it's still early, and it's not very hot."

Liburna was a large fishing village built very close to the sea, and at that hour in the morning it was semi-deserted. On the sides of the large road that divided the village into two parts, there were many stalls with goods on display: cheese, onions, wool, tools for working and cooking, and, above all, for fishing.

Raterio felt compelled to give some explanation to the two young people accompanying him. 'Today there are not many people...most of the inhabitants are fishermen, and they are at sea until tonight. Do you see those nets?" he continued, pointing to a young girl sitting on a bench by the side of the road who was sewing one up with a large wooden needle "they are for catching fish. They get in there, and are no longer able to get out. So the fishermen pull them into the boat and empty them. Then they throw them out again. Sometimes they break by rubbing against the sea bed, and that's why they have to be sewn up again."

Riccardo was reminded of Edoardo's tales of sea monsters: terrible snakes that could eat large ships full of men at once, huge octopuses that were the terror of sailors. Perhaps it was the monsters that broke the nets.

"Now," said Raterio, "I have to go to someone's place to buy some things...in the meantime you can take a walk around the village. Look there...see that red sign? It's an Inn. We'll meet there at sunset, when the sun is slowly sinking into the sea. It's an unforgettable sight." The blacksmith departed, leaving Riccardo and Celeste overjoyed to be able to explore together, for a whole day, that world full of surprises.

1998

Home at last! Five days in the hospital... unbelievable stuff. They had turned him inside out; they had done every possible and imaginable analysis, from the stool analysis to the AIDS test; the only thing out of place was a slight increase in his maximum cholesterol levels: everything else was in perfect order.
He had spoken to a dermatologist, a neurologist and a psychiatrist. Of course, he had not told anyone about his strange visions, also because they had not recurred; neither had the sweating.
The headache had passed, and now he only felt a slight soreness all over his body.
Marta had driven him home, and then gone to a dentist's appointment, but at dinner time she would be there again. She was so dear and thoughtful! On the way back she would stop and buy the necessary items to prepare a wonderful dinner, and he knew very well that Marta cooked exceptionally well. Maybe one day he would ask her to move in with him. Maybe. He was afraid she might refuse.

Roberto was a native of Valdinievole, Pescia to be exact, but had had to move to Livorno for work reasons. His flat was on the ground floor and was reduced to the bare minimum: a bedroom, a living room-kitchen and a bathroom; then, of course, there was the computer room with which, because of the Internet and thanks to his more than fair knowledge of English, he was in contact with the whole world.
He glanced at the grandfather clock on the wall and noticed that it was stopped at eleven forty on who knows what day. It was the inheritance of an old

aunt, an object from the early 1900s that he was very fond of. He climbed onto a chair and wound it up; then he turned the hands to strike the hours; when he reached six o'clock, he started the pendulum. The ticking immediately put him in a good mood, and he began to whistle, using the clock's tic-tac as a metronome.

He turned on the television and tuned in the Discovery Channel, his favourite programme. He immediately realised that something was wrong: the pictures were showing, but there was no sound. They were broadcasting a documentary. Roberto tried unsuccessfully to turn up the volume, then tried to change the channel, but nothing happened. He threw the remote control on the sofa and went to his room to undress.

Maybe they're out of batteries for the remote control...I have to phone Marta to get some. And let's hope it's the batteries, otherwise it will take a lot of money to get the television fixed. Now that was all we needed.

Completely naked, he put on his slippers and headed for the shower, but his attention was drawn to the images that were passing at that moment on the television screen.

It was a faithful reconstruction of a medieval village, perfect in every detail, and made even more realistic by the use of a hand held camera used at face height, so that the viewer had the impression of seeing everything around him with his own eyes. The documentary was shot in high definition, and an amber coloured filter added warmth to the whole scene. But the thing that really struck Roberto were the actors who played the villagers: the director had found incredible faces, perfectly in tune with the reconstruction. And they were very good: hardly anyone looked at the camera, and those who did have such a natural air that made the performance worthy of an Oscar.

I wonder if there is an Oscar for this kind of documentary ...

When even the last houses of the village had been overtaken, the camera abruptly shifted its range, and framed a beach so barren and wild that Roberto wondered where such a beautiful and unspoilt place could be.

Perhaps it was filmed in Corsica. Or maybe Sardegna.

Suddenly the framing changed, and for Roberto it was like a punch in the stomach.

The woman dressed as a monk was looking at him and smiling; then she approached the camera, stepped out of the television and kissed him.

The woman's tongue crept into Roberto's mouth, and he stood in the middle of the room, paralysed with terror, as that quivering body rubbed vigorously against his nakedness.

Then the woman broke away, went back inside the television and started running towards the sea.

Roberto threw himself on the sofa, frantically grabbed the remote control and switched off the device. The LED changed from green to red, but that was the only change.

Now the camera was chasing the woman.

With a leap, he reached for the power plug of the device and pulled it forcefully out of the wall.

Nothing. The camera had almost reached the woman, who was standing with her feet in the water and smiling.

Then he let out a scream and fled into the shower. He closed the plastic door of the cabin and turned on the cold water tap, shivering under that icy jet.
He then had an incredible erection again.
He stood still for a couple of minutes, unable to think; then he turned on the hot water tap until an acceptable temperature was reached. He got out, put on his bathrobe and walked over to the television. There were no more pictures. He breathed a sigh of relief and went back to the shower again.
His eyes began to sting and he realised with amazement that the water was salty.

1065

They found themselves at the Inn, as arranged.
Raterio had with him a bag containing two stones for sharpening scythes; sometimes for this purpose he used some stones he collected near his village, but apart from the disappointing results, the stones crumbled easily, making the operation somewhat dangerous. More than once he had cut himself, and on the back of his left hand he was left with a rather conspicuous scar.
This stone, on the other hand, was very hard, sharpened scythes and knives beautifully and lasted a long time. The last time he had bought one was a couple of years ago; this time he had bought two, so he would not need to return to Liburna for a long time.
It had become increasingly common to bring scythes and knives to him for sharpening. Until recently, farmers had done this themselves, but they had gradually realised that a scythe that cut better lasted longer and made people sweat less, so it had to be sharpened by a professional.
Raterio was a much sought after blacksmith, and people knew that he worked well and was honest.
His customers were not only the villagers where he lived, but many also came from neighbouring villages; when the work required Rateric, it was he who went to the place, and stayed there until he had finished it.

They entered a smoke filled room and sat down on a bench that wobbled frighteningly, resting their elbows on a table that was completely empty, but as filthy as the steps of a chicken coop.

What was most striking upon entering the Inn was the strong smell of boiled cabbage, which seemed to come directly from the walls of the room; and in part this was the truth, for the wooden planks of which they were constructed must surely have been impregnated with all the various aromas that had alternated in the kitchen over the years.

The room consisted of three large tables with benches occupying almost the entire room and a decrepit fireplace leaning against the back wall. The fireplace was high off the ground, so that it also served as a kitchen, and an incredible amount of pots and pans, of all shapes and sizes, had been attached to its side walls. A woman of indefinable age was busy stirring with a long ladle the contents of a pitch black pot that smoked like a green grass fire.

The Innkeeper, a man in his thirties with an abominable belly, was lighting two torches attached to a wall; as soon as he saw the three new patrons sitting down, he assessed them with an expert eye.

He immediately realised that they had brought nothing to eat. Those three were luxury customers.

Usually his customers brought their own bread and wine; so they paid a pittance for the seat they occupied, and stayed there getting drunk late into the night.

He wrinkled his plump hands with satisfaction, and approached the table.

"Hello. What can I do for you?" he said, giving the table a quick rub with a cloth so greasy you couldn't even tell what colour it was.

"We want to eat something," replied Raterio, "and then we would also like a place to spend the night."

The Innkeeper smiled.

"All right, there is everything. Tonight my wife made cabbage soup, then, if you want, I can bring you boiled fish. For sleeping there is a spare room just behind that wall. You'll find fresh straw there. If anything escapes you during the night, go out the window, which is very low, and go behind the house. There you will find a hole...be careful, because at night it is easy to fall in."

The Innkeeper stood waiting with folded arms, satisfied that he had set out so clearly all the services his Inn could offer.

"We always eat cabbage soup," said Raterio, "No soup. Bring the boiled fish, and let it be plentiful. We also want bread, a tray of salad and light beer."

"Good. We also have honey pastries..."

"We'll see. In the meantime, bring the other stuff."

Celeste was stunned by all the news. Like Riccardo, it was the first time she had ever eaten in an Inn. In her village there was one, but she had never set foot in it in her life; it was frequented only by people passing through.

The sunset had been beautiful.

Riccardo and Celeste had seen it embraced, sitting by the same rock on which they had arrived that morning: and in the cool of the pines they had made love. And afterwards they had undressed completely and entered the water.

The spectacle of the sun slowly descending into the sea until it turned red and then disappeared into the water had made the two lovers accomplices in this exceptional event, tightening even more the bond of love that bound them together.

The fish, salad and bread arrived; the Innkeeper also brought three earthenware mugs and a pitcher of beer, which seemed dark to Raterio, but he did not feel the need to argue.

All three ate with appetite, drank all the beer and had another jug brought. The landlord of the Inn also insisted that they try his honeyed pastries, and Raterio, who was a very greedy man, ate them greedily, wiping away with his fingertips even the crumbs that remained at the bottom of the wooden bowl.

Riccardo often ate fish: behind his village ran a stream, where, when the water was low, he would go to catch prey with a spear of his own invention. He would tie together three pointed poles of the same length; then, a palm's width from the tips, he would wedge two pieces of wood to hold them apart.

The system worked very well: he would lift a stone, and nail the victim to the rhine bottom of the stream with his three-pronged spear. He would bring it home, and his mother would roast it directly over the fire or boil it. Immediately afterwards his father would arrive, eat, drink wine until he was drunk, and beat them both.

"Did you like the fish?" Celeste's voice woke him from those bad thoughts.

"Yes, it was very good. I often ate fish from the stream, but those from the sea are tastier. Besides, they are bigger," replied Riccardo.

"Now let's go and rest; tomorrow morning I want to leave before the sun rises. In this season we walk better if it is not yet very hot." said Raterio.

"What will you do?" intervened Celeste with a hint of anxiety in her voice.

"I don't know yet...I think I will accompany you for a stretch, then I will decide," replied Riccardo.

At that moment a dozen or so patrons entered the Inn, and amid laughter and cackling they sat down at the table next to them; they were all about Raterio's age, and from the stench they emanated one could tell at once that they were fishermen.

"Teofano!" called the oldest of the bunch in an authoritative voice, "bring us four or five jugs of wine...and if I find a single drop of water in them, I swear I'll put an apple in your mouth, stick a stick up your ass, and roast you over a fire like a pig!"

"But you don't have to worry," resumed another of the patrons, "we'll give you a turn, so you won't get too hot!"

Naturally, the two jokes were greeted by a general burst of laughter, which also involved Riccardo and Raterio; Celeste also laughed, but in a more composed manner.

Suddenly one of the group members stood up and approached Raterio: "But you are not Raterio? Raterio, the son of Hugh the smith?"

As soon as he heard him speak, he recognised him immediately. He was a childhood friend whom he had not seen for at least fifteen years. A native of his village, he had left with his two brothers in search of fortune after a terrible fire had destroyed their home.

"Egisto! By all the devils, I thought you were dead and buried!" replied Raterio, arousing further laughter among those present.

"Dead? Well, if I am dead you had better die too, for I have never been so well in my life!" said Egisto laughing.

"And your brothers? I don't see them here with you...are they well?"

An unreal silence fell over those present.

"Last year...a storm. We were together, and I was the only one saved..."

"I'm sorry, I didn't know." whispered Raterio futilely trying to find something else to say.

"Now now, no more melancholy!" resumed Egisto vigorously, turning to those present, "let us all drink together to the friendship that binds me to this man! If you knew how much we got up to when we were young..."

"Why don't we elect your friend king of the party?" said one of those present.

"Yes!" exclaimed Egisto, "that's a very good idea!"

"Actually, I have to get up early tomorrow..." objected Raterio with little conviction.

"Get up? You'll get up if you go to sleep!" said Egisto laughing, "Otherwise you'll already be up!"

The Innkeeper brought five jugs of wine and mugs for everyone; someone took out a crown woven from willows and leaves, and the feast began.

The King of the Feast was a very fashionable custom in those days.

During a particularly merry evening, one of those present had a crown put on his head, usually made of laurel or other leaves; he was the King, and everything he did was to be imitated by those present. When the King drank the others drank, when the King sang the others sang, when the King went to piss the others followed him and pissed along with him.

The purpose of this amusement was to drink as much as possible, and to accompany each other home, drunk as drunk as could be, singing and squawking as much as possible.

The Innkeepers had much to gain from this game, as wine and beer flowed freely. After the first few times, they had learned to get paid in advance to avoid unpleasant disputes with customers.

There was, it is true, the flip side of the coin: if the king was too violent and broke something, everyone else imitated him, and soon all that was left of the bar was a pile of splintered wood and a few pieces of terracotta on which the Innkeeper sat and mourned his misfortunes.

Celeste and Riccardo moved to a corner and prepared to enjoy the unusual evening.

Above all, Celeste saw her father in an unusual version; he drank, told stories that made the members of the group burst out laughing, sang the most vulgar of traditional Tuscany songs at the top of his voice; but the climax of the fun was when he told them that his friend Egidio, while picking olives on a rather tall tree, had become entangled in a branch; trying to free himself, he had fallen, but his robe had torn, and he had come to the ground completely naked before the astonished eyes of the women who were picking olives at the foot of the tree. One child had seen him and exclaimed, 'Look, Mama! It's bigger than daddy's!"

He had run away in shame, but soon that story had become public knowledge in the small village.

They drank eleven jugs of wine; then they said goodbye and left the Inn singing.

Raterio got up and said, "The King is going to sleep!" He took two steps and fell ruinously to the ground; Riccardo and Celeste made a tremendous effort to drag him to the room adjoining the kitchen, which was lit only by the faint glow of the moonlight coming in through the window. When their eyes had become accustomed to the semi darkness, they saw fresh straw in a corner, and placed Raterio there; then they lay down beside each other, and took each other's hands, shaking them tightly. Raterio saw them out of the corner of his eye, but he was too drunk to think; he turned away and fell asleep.

The two young people also fell asleep at once, and Riccardo dreamt that he was in the middle of the sea in a small boat, just as the sun was setting; the boat was exactly in the middle of the red wake, and was speeding towards the sun. He was standing, his three-pronged spear firmly in his right hand, carefully scanning the sea in the hope of seeing some fish. But suddenly the sea ran out, and Riccardo sank with his boat into an endless well.

1998

Roberto woke up suddenly and touched his forehead: it was dripping with sweat. He turned on the light and sat up in bed. His heart was beating wildly, and it took several minutes before it resumed its normal rhythm. *Maybe I exaggerated... I must not eat so much, especially in the evening... but it was all so good!*

Other times he had had dreams about falling into the void, especially when he was a child; but he always woke up before he hit the bottom. This time it had been different.
An interminable flight, a free fall into absolute emptiness; he could see the stars shining, in the distance, but he couldn't recognise any of the constellations. He was falling.
He fell into an abyss that erased all memories, names, faces; he fell into a timeless space, he fell into a barrel of sticky black pitch that seemed to have no end. But then it did end, and Roberto stepped into a clear sea, so green it took his breath away; he went down, deeper and deeper, gazing enchanted at the vivid colours of all those fish circling around him. But the wonder was short-lived, giving way to terror: that beautiful green sea had suddenly turned into thick, viscous honey, and he could no longer move. He was like a fossil crystallised inside a huge amber coloured mass.

The dinner had been fabulous. And the after dinner had been fabulous too. Marta had prepared incredibly good crabmeat dumplings and he had gratified her by eating two full plates. Then he had

devoured an incredible amount of swordfish carpaccio and salmon, accompanying it all with a bottle of Vermentino '92 that he kept for special occasions. And this was indeed a special occasion.
"Damn!" Marta had exclaimed, "They really didn't give you anything to eat at the hospital!"
"No, I ate...but everything was so anonymous, everything was so the same. And then tonight I had a craving for fish...I would have eaten it even raw."
When dinner was over, Marta had asked how he was feeling, and Roberto had finally decided to confide in her.
He had told her everything, from the apparition of that strange woman dressed as a monk to the most embarrassing moment at the hospital, with his wife standing there.
When he then told her that at that very moment his wife had asked him if he was ill, Marta burst out laughing.
She had an engaging way of laughing, and soon Roberto imitated her. They both found themselves laughing to tears at a fact that five minutes earlier had seemed like a nightmare to Roberto; but now, thanks to those few moments of serenity, he had managed to play it down a little.
The intimacy of those revelations made the shyness they felt for each other disappear, and those two quivering bodies finally sought each other out and found each other in a shattering embrace, one of those you remember all your life.
Then Marta, around one o'clock, had returned to her house, telling Roberto that she did not yet feel ready to stay there all night in his bed; he had been a little disappointed, but he understood her, and had

consoled himself by convincing himself that it was only a matter of time.

Marta's life had not been easy: she came from an orphanage, and this had undoubtedly affected her entire adolescence and part of her youth.
When she came of age, an uncle who had suddenly become a widower at the age of fifty-six, with no children or other relatives, decided to take her with him to his home in Livorno, and Marta was overjoyed to be able to leave the orphanage and finally begin to lead a normal life; not that she was ill-treated by the nuns, on the contrary: but the world was outside those walls.
Uncle Carlo was really good: always caring, he loved Marta like a daughter, and she loved him back with enthusiasm, continually thanking the Lord for letting her find this splendid relative.
Uncle Carlo did not want Marta to work: he had a very good pension and some money to spare, and was content for her to perform the duties of a housewife; and Marta gladly accommodated him, keeping the house as polished as a mirror and cooking excellently.
Four wonderful years passed, until Marta found the love of her life in a man she met at the theatre.
She had been invited by an actress friend of hers to see the rehearsal of a play that her company was preparing for a festival to be held at the Verdi Theatre in Pisa; the play, a script by Aldo De Benedetti entitled 'From Thursday to Thursday', was really good, and the actors, although all amateurs, were really good.
That experience fascinated her so much that she was convinced by her friend to join the company as a

costume designer, and she began reading everything she could find on the subject.

After three months, she fell in love with Claudio, the set designer of the group, who felt the same, and after another seven months they decided to get married, also because Marta was pregnant.

Two weeks before the wedding, Claudio took Marta's uncle, who had no car, for an eye examination at the hospital in Pisa.

They never returned. A lorry travelling in the opposite direction to them on the Aurelia suddenly skidded and ran over their car. They both died instantly, amidst the screams of the truck driver and the twisted metal sheets of the car.

Following this terrible misfortune Marta had decided to have an abortion; unlike what most women would have thought, she did not feel like raising a child who would inevitably remind her of Claudio.

Afterwards, she had begun to hate herself for that perhaps too rash choice, and from then on always tried to avoid places where mothers took their children to play.

That decision had also affected her character, making her insecure about everything; when it came to making a choice, Marta thought about it not once, but a hundred times, even if it was to buy a pair of socks.

There had been no more men in her life, and she had begun to hate cars; then, in time, she had become a convinced ecologist and had met Roberto.

Marta did not love Roberto, but she liked him because he was strong, self-confident, in short he was everything she could no longer be.

Roberto's only flaw was his job: the mere thought that he was constantly in contact with children made her sick.

But she had no one else, and she had clung on to him to try to get out of that whirlwind of memories that overwhelmed her emotionally; and Roberto had often helped her, trying to make that little blond child who appeared in her dreams almost every night disappear with tranquillity and cheerfulness.

Absorbed in velvety thoughts of the evening spent with Marta, and certain that the visions and disturbances he had been subjected to would never again be a problem, Roberto got out of bed to go to the bathroom; he crossed the kitchen, placed a chair in front of the window, climbed over it and urinated on the white daisies in the flowerbed behind the house.

1065

They set off early in the morning, and walked briskly until the sun was right above them; they stopped near a stream, and after cooling off and drinking, they sat down in the shade of a huge chestnut tree to rest for a while. Riccardo assessed that stream with an expert's eye, decided that there must be some fish there, and went into a grove a stone's throw from the bank. He returned almost immediately with three thin poles and a few willow twigs. He pinned the poles with his knife, tied them together and constructed his famous spear. Under the watchful eyes of Raterio and the languid ones of Celeste he took off his sandals and slowly entered the stream. He lifted four stones without success; on the fifth attempt, a rather large trout darted out and tried to swim upstream: but Riccardo's spear nailed it hopelessly to the bottom of the stream. He repeated the operation several times, always moving upstream: in the end he had managed to catch three medium-sized trout, which Celeste roasted over the fire previously lit by her father. They ate with gusto, regretting only that they had no beer or wine: they had to make do with the fresh water flowing next to them.

Riccardo, lying in the shade of the chestnut tree, could not take his eyes off the serene face of Celeste, who was sleeping soundly with her head resting on a pile of leaves. By now he had realised that he loved her, and would do anything to live with her. Being a bright young man he also realised that Raterio would be overjoyed by this union.

He had no emotional attachment to the country of his birth; therefore, he could decide on his life as he saw fit.

It troubled him somewhat that he had not been faithful to his principles: he had left to see the sea, and in his heart he hoped that he would stay there to live, perhaps as a fisherman, or perhaps repairing nets.

But now another prospect opened up before him: that of being with Celeste forever, having children, and helping Raterio in his work as a blacksmith. He knew he would succeed, also because learning to work iron fascinated him.

He approached Raterio, who was absorbed in watching the flowing water.

"Excuse me...I would like to ask you a question," he said.

"Go ahead." smiled Raterio at him.

"Celeste, your daughter...is she promised to someone?"

"I guessed it was Celeste. I saw how you look at each other...do you want to take her away from me?"

"No...take away no...I would like to learn blacksmithing, and I was wondering if you needed a helper."

"I get it...you can read minds! Come, let's wake up my daughter. If she's happy with what you've told me, then I'll be happy too," Raterio concluded, already thinking about how to enlarge the house and make it suitable for this pleasant novelty.

They woke Celeste, and Riccardo informed her of the facts, making her cry with joy. Then they all three set off on their way home, aware that this happiness was only the prelude to a peaceful and quiet life that was opening up before them.

Chapter Two

Vineland, New Jersey, USA.
March 2000

...Memories. So many memories. A trip to America. Vineland, New York, Philadelphia... skyscrapers, taxis, people, people. Living. Finally living. Building the puzzle over a gelatinous board of liquefied amber. Connecting the pieces. Connect the lives. In an orderly way. Or even randomly, it doesn't matter. The important thing is to connect, to unite. To go on living.

1

It had been raining for many days now, and water had begun to pour out of the saturated fields and invade the streets of the town. People were reluctantly moving from their homes, and televisions were running at full capacity throughout the state. Of course, the most popular programme was the one where the weather forecast was announced, but there was little hope that it would stop raining in the short term, so the accusations sent to the various presenters were endless.

According to the old timers, a season like this had never been seen before: some blamed the greenhouse effect, others the fact that the year two thousand had just begun, and others took refuge in the usual cliché *that there are no longer any half seasons.*

It was eight o'clock on a Sunday morning, and Elaine was on her way to the kitchen to fry up some bacon for breakfast, when the phone rang; still half asleep, she abruptly changed direction and headed for the telephone.

Elaine Giuliani was the only daughter of a Tuscany shoemaker who immigrated to America, along with many other Italians, in the 1950s.

Her father's great dream was to find a good job, start a family and be able to afford a large, comfortable home. Practically the dream of all emigrants who had decided to leave their homeland.

After various adventures, her father had managed to set up a small shoe factory that gave him a good living.

It was at that time that he found Sandy, an American girl with a big round face like the moon and eyes as black as night, and fell in love with her at first sight; after eight months they were already husband and wife.

In 1968 they decided that perhaps a child was needed, and a year later a delightful little girl with her father's features and her mother's eyes was born.

The father wanted to call her Elena, but the mother said that there was already an Italian surname, so they didn't even think about it; they ended up agreeing on Elaine.

When, in the 1970s, Made-in-Italy made a strong foothold in the new world, Mr. Giuliani was already able to produce about sixty pairs of shoes a day, and employed eleven factory workers and about fifteen who worked off the books.

Every day Sandy went to the factory with her husband, taking the baby with her, and when the baby was hungry, she shamelessly breastfed her in front of the workers.

Of course Elaine soon became the mascot of the factory, and everyone cuddled her, also because she had learnt to be loved, and when Mario, the foreman, tickled him, her crystal clear laughter covered even the noise of the machinery. The shoes that came out of the factory were marked Made in Italy.

Mr Giuliani did not consider this a fraud, because if it was true that they were made in the USA, it was equally true that all the material, including the cardboard for the models and the nails for the soles, came from Italy.

He had a friend in Monsummano who punctually sent him everything he needed; of course Mr. Giuliani knew that this friend charged a bit too much, but he didn't care.

'Better to spend a few dollars more and get quality stuff, than a few dollars less and have your shoes open when it rains,' he used to say.

In 1990, having accumulated a nice little nest egg, he had started the construction of his new house, which would allow him a well deserved rest after fifty years of work.

It was a three-storey house, with a large park and a swimming pool that Mr. Giuliani had wanted in the shape of an 'E' like the initial of his daughter's name.

But just one month after the completion of the work, Mr. Giuliani left this valley of tears forever.

The tragic event took place in August 1992, right on the birthday of Elaine, who was twenty-three years old on that day and who had wanted to celebrate this event in her new home.

The grounds of the villa were full of guests: there were workers from the shoe factory with their families, representatives and various political personalities whom Mr. Giuliani had met in the course of his life, whether for business or politics.

The band had just begun to play a cheerful march and Sandy was carrying a huge puff pastry cake full of candles from the kitchen, when Mr. Giuliani slumped to the ground, slowly, without a groan.

Fulminating heart attack was the conclusion of the doctor who was immediately called and arrived within minutes.

Two months later, Sandy also died, just like her husband, and Elaine found herself alone, without a single relative, facing a life that, after having pampered her for her first twenty-three years, had finally shown its true face.

But she did not lose heart, strengthened by the character she had inherited from her parents who wanted her to be at the top at all costs: she sold the shoe factory to a large corporation, making almost a million and a half dollars, and began to make her history degree pay off, buying a small building in New York, near the Metropolitan Museum, and opening a consulting firm right on her doorstep.

It was in this way that she began to appreciate that great city: she loved the hurried people who passed by it as they walked on the pavements of the great streets, she loved the rivers of yellow taxis that seemed to be in perpetual procession, she loved the glittering lights of the shops, she loved the glitz and elegance of the shop windows run by the big names.

But most of all, she loved Central Park, with its wonderful paths full of squirrels that took her back in her mind to her Vineland.

She had kept the house, a perennial reminder of her parents, and she liked to think that every time she returned she would find it still there, welcoming her as warmly as ever.

She had made a habit of spending weekends in New Jersey; she would leave in her car on Friday evening and return to New York on Monday morning, in time for the afternoon reopening. After all, she was not bound by particularly strict timetables, as most clients came to her by appointment.

She also finally found love.

Many had been her suitors in her youth, and after all, it couldn't be any other way: she was beautiful, rich and nice. But of all these probable boyfriends, not one had proved equal to the task, and she had found herself celebrating her 26th birthday still as unblemished and pure as a lily.

Then came Pedro Cortez, a noble Spanish heartthrob as handsome as the sun, who had enchanted her with his Latin charm. After three months, they were married, and almost immediately he started cheating on her with an old flame of his that he had never completely got rid of.

After a year of marriage, Elaine had to go to a school in Philadelphia to give a lecture on the life and works of Niccolò Machiavelli, and on the way back she stopped at a café on the highway to rest a little. She got out of the car, entered the bar and ordered an orange juice. She sat down near the front door, from where, through a large window, she could see the two lanes of the motorway.

She looked absent mindedly at the passing cars, and after a couple of minutes, to her surprise she saw the car she had given Pedro five months earlier.

Elaine recognised it immediately, because of a yellow band across the sides.

Of course it was Pedro behind the wheel, and next to him sat that breathtaking blonde Wanda.

The car proceeded slowly: he put on his indicator, exited the motorway, passed the bar and headed for the Ramada Motel that bordered the place where she was sitting.

From her position, Elaine could not see the hotel entrance, so she got up, paid quickly and got out in time to catch Pedro and Wanda walking hand in hand towards the entrance.

She dropped onto a providential wooden bench and sat for a good half hour, holding her face in her hands and giving a quick, bitter recap of her love life. Then she got up sharply, got into her car, drove into the car park of the Ramada Motel and drove into the back of her husband's car. She then got out, went to the reception desk and called the owner of the metallic BMW parked outside, in order to pay for the damage. The young lady on duty was very helpful: not only did she tell her that the car belonged to Mr. Pedro Cortez, a regular customer of the hotel, but also that he was currently in room 216 with his wife, and that she would inform him immediately.

After five minutes, Pedro came down the stairs, accompanied by Wanda. The comical side of the matter was that Elaine, who was waiting behind a pillar so that she could not be seen, heard Pedro say to the woman:

"Let's hope it's nothing serious...it's a gift from my wife...who knows how angry she'll be when I tell her!"

Elaine had not opened her mouth; she had come out from behind the pillar, and had stopped in front of them. The two of them stared at her dumbfounded under the wide-eyed eyes of the young lady at the reception desk, who hadn't understood a thing.

They had never spoken to each other again. The whole thing had been put in the hands of lawyers, and after two years she had finally managed to get a divorce, spending nearly forty thousand dollars. She had sworn to herself that she would never again succumb to the flattery of a man, especially one of Latin blood.

"Hello?"

On the other end of the phone a deep voice asked, "Is this Miss Giuliani? Elaine Giuliani?"

"It's me, tell me."

"Listen, we don't know each other... my name is Francesco Zimbaldi, and I teach history at the classical high school in Livorno, Italy. This phone number was given to me by Professor Smith, who told me to contact you for a research paper I am about to undertake..."

"Ah, Professor Ferdinand Smith!" said Elaine, reprimanding her old friend for giving someone that phone number she considered confidential.

Ferdinand Smith was one of the foremost scholars of medieval history, and was considered by insiders to be a veritable well of knowledge; but Elaine hated talking about work on her weekends, and even more hated talking about it at eight o'clock in the morning before breakfast.

"Tell me, what can I do for you?"

"I was told that you have a historical consulting office... is that correct?"

"That is correct."

"I'd like to make an appointment, so I can explain the details to you verbally...in the afternoon, if you don't

mind...Professor Smith tells me you are well versed in medieval Italian history."
"It's not exactly my specific field, but I get by...my father was Italian, so I know the language well, and that helps me a lot. Is Tuesday afternoon at four o'clock ok for you?"
"Yes, Tuesday at four. Professor Smith w ll accompany me, so you don't need to give me the address. Goodbye."
"Goodbye." said Elaine, hanging up the phone.
It was a very strange thing. Professor Smith, a university lecturer in medieval history, was immensely learned, and he certainly knew a lot more about the subject than she did... unless he was trying to dump a job he didn't like on her. But no, he wasn't that type.
But then, what was the job for which she had been asked? Maybe her client was writing a book... very often they called on her to check the historical reliability of the texts. But on the phone he said it was a job he was about to undertake...
All right, all right... Elaine, curb your usual curiosity. Wait until Tuesday and then you'll know everything precisely... in the meantime, how would you like a nice, hearty breakfast?

2

The sun was shining in New York and the skyscrapers were shining against the blue sky; only over there, to the south-east, could one glimpse the black clouds that were still pouring streams of water over the state of New Jersey.

The journey had not been the most pleasant: the heavy rain that had accompanied Elaine most of the way had made visibility very poor, and when the rain had stopped the splashing of cars, but especially trucks, had annoyed her not a little.

She pulled into the usual underground car park at second street level, parked her car, took the lift and when she was on the pavement she hailed a taxi.

Elaine had a chronic habit. Fanatical about punctuality, more than once she had denied herself to clients who were more than twenty minutes late for an appointment.

In fact, twenty minutes seemed too long, but she realised that she was in a hectic city, where the unexpected is always just around the corner.

To get around New York she almost always used taxis, much more rarely buses; she didn't even want to hear about the underground.

She was afraid: too many strange things were happening on the New York underground, and even though Mayor Giuliani had now managed to drastically reduce crime, he was not to be trusted too much. Elaine's surname was also Giuliani, but they were not related. Who knows, but perhaps they came from the same stock; after all, they both came from Tuscany.

She had made an arrangement with the owner of the garage where she left her car, and had even persuaded him to keep the usual place for her. It had not even cost her much.

Elaine wasn't stingy, but she was careful about how she spent her money; she didn't let herself want for anything, and although she had invested something like a million dollars in stocks and shares, which yielded her about ten per cent a year, she lived soberly, and never flaunted her wealth in front of others, especially when she was in the presence of people she knew to be less well off than herself.

On the other hand, she was well aware that her job would never allow her to have the standard of living she currently enjoyed.

She had graduated in history at a very young age, and had also taken a course in archaeology, but had never finished it, because she had realised that to delve deeper into that science she would have to travel.

And she had never been on a plane in her life.

It was not simple fear, but real terror; many times she had proposed to take a trip, perhaps a short one, but at the last moment she had always given up. She had only one friend, also of Italian origin: Linda Cerrasi.

Linda was a retired mathematics teacher. Despite her completely Italian name, she did not know a single word of the Italian language. Her father and mother, of Sicilian origin, had never spoken Italian since they had immigrated to America. To learn the local language they took a very expensive course, so at home they preferred to speak in English, so as well as saving money on lessons, they were able to study on their own.

Linda was very fat, but she did not show her fifty-six years at all. She had taught twenty-six years in Boston at a public school, then, after her husband's death in a car accident, she had given it all up and bought a small house right next to Elaine's office.

She had no children, and her affection was completely devoted to cats, for whom she had an almost deep passion. She currently owned three, but in her heyday she was known to have as many as seven. She had her small garden fenced off with a very high net, in the hope that her beloved cats would not be able to go into the street; but sometimes they managed to climb over, and inevitably ended up under some car.

In 1997, Minnie, her favourite cat, had decided that the prison was too small for her, and after several unsuccessful attempts, she managed to leave.

Linda had cried for two whole days, then, when all hope had faded, Elaine found Minnie locked up in her office and returned her to her rightful owner. Thus was born a deep friendship, made even stronger by the fact that the two women were in no way romantically linked.

The taxi took about fifteen minutes to get her home; there was never much traffic on a Monday morning at that time.

Elaine paid the taxi driver the eight dollars he demanded, got out, took the mail out of the box at the side of the gate and gave it a quick look; then she opened the gate and walked down the gravel driveway to the front door; she threw it open and entered the large living room; she lit a cigarette, put her purse on the table and headed for her room, happy to finally be able to undress and take a relaxing whirlpool bath.

3

And finally Tuesday arrived.

Elaine was impatient to hear from Professor Smith why he had pointed her out to that Italian teacher; she had tried twice to phone him, but had never found him at home.

It had already been ten minutes past four o'clock, and Elaine, true to her character, was already beginning to get impatient, when the glass door to the office swung open and Professor Smith entered, followed by his Italian friend.

Francesco Zimbaldi was forty-six years old, and he took great care of his image, even if mother nature didn't give him a hand: he was about 1.60 metres tall, with a big squashed nose that didn't make him at all attractive; long but sparse reddish hair started from behind his ears and went down to his shoulders, while a thick, white spotted beard completed the picture.

Zimbaldi was gay, but he had great difficulty admitting it. No one knew it, except perhaps his younger brother, to whom he was very close; but he, a Breda worker, lived in Pistoia with his family, and they rarely saw each other.

Zimbaldi taught history at Livorno's classical high school, although on more than one occasion he had the chance to make the leap and join the University of Pisa as a lecturer: but he had always given up, because for years he had been secretly in love with Luca, a penniless guitarist who lived by giving music lessons.

He had seen him for the first time at a rock concert in Vada, in the seventies: Luca was playing with a band from Arezzo, and his long, thin fingers moving fast on the neck of the dark mahogany Gibson Diavoletto had literally driven him crazy.

Tall and blond, Luca on this occasion wore a red shirt open to the navel, pinched at the waist by a black leather belt at least ten centimetres high; a gold like metal buckle and fashionable ankle boots completed the ensemble.

It had been a thunderbolt: he had continued to watch him all evening, even when he came off-stage and other groups were performing.

Finally, Luca, intrigued by the fact that this strange guy kept staring at him, had approached him.

"Hi, do we happen to know each other?" he had said to Francesco, who with his heart in his throat had stammered "No... that is, yes... actually... I thought... I thought you were a friend of mine from Livorno... excuse me..."

"From Livorno?" the young man had exclaimed, "I live in Livorno too! What's your friend's name? Does he play the guitar? Maybe I know him!"

That was how it had started, with that strange friendship born of embarrassment; to see him more often, Francesco had started taking guitar lessons from Luca. This had continued for two years, until Luca had found himself a beautiful girl and married her.

Francesco had spent three months in complete depression, despising himself for never having had the courage to reveal his love to Luca; yet there had been plenty of opportunities to do so... but then he had decided it was better that way, knowing that with such a move the friendship between him and the object of his desires would inevitably be compromised.

Thirty years had now passed, Luca was a night watchman; he had put on some weight and besides having a few white hairs he also had two children. But Francesco's love had remained unchanged, and he would continue to love him in silence for the rest of his life.

"Hello Elaine...I would like to introduce you to Dr Francesco Zimbaldi. You two have already met by phone." said Smith.
"It's a real pleasure, Miss...The Professor has spoken so highly of you that I've been looking forward to meeting you," Zimbaldi said in perfect English, shaking her hand.
"Good. If you would like to take a seat..." Elaine pointed to the chairs in front of the desk. The two sat down, after which Smith began to speak.
"Well, Elaine, listen... first of all, I owe you an apology for bothering you over the weekend. I know how much you value your privacy, but you know me, and you know I would never have called unless it was really an urgent case. Zimbaldi has been here in New York since Saturday, but he'll only be here a short time. Tonight at eight p.m. he has the plane that will take him back to Italy."
"I see." said Elaine, "What can I do for you?"
"It wouldn't hurt to start telling the facts from the beginning," said Francesco Zimbaldi, then cleared his throat and began to speak calmly.
"I met Professor Smith at a medieval history conference in Rome last summer. I knew very well who he was, because all of us history scholars know that there is no man in the world more knowledgeable on the subject than him, so I did my best to approach him. I thought I was facing an event

that was as exceptional as it was inexplicable, but I wanted to talk to an expert on the subject first. Professor Smith's deductions confirmed my thesis, and from then on we began a close collaboration made up mostly of e-mails and long telephone calls." Then Zimbaldi cleared his throat again, giving the impression that he had something important to say, and continued "There is a man, in Livorno, who has the ability to describe, with disconcerting exactness of detail, the lives of some people who lived in the Middle Ages." There was a moment's pause. Elaine's gaze met the eyes of an impassive Smith, and Zimbaldi continued. "I realise that said like this might sound crazy, but I assure you it is the pure truth. The name of the subject in question is Roberto Birindelli. I first met him in November 1998 through my niece Marta, who had approached me more for advice than anything else. I went to the address she gave me, and after seeing Roberto and talking to him for a good two hours straight, not a single day went by that I didn't think about looking into this further matter."

Elaine smiled almost imperceptibly. Too many times she had been confronted with such situations to be able to take the matter seriously; but Smith knew her well.

"Elaine, I assure you that there is nothing exaggerated or untrue in what Dr Zimbaldi has told you; he is merely reporting the reality to you, as he saw it and as I also saw it three months ago during my trip to Italy. This Roberto Birindelli underwent CT scans, MRI scans and tests to prove his actual mental faculties. Everything turned out to be in order, and he passed all the tests brilliantly. But make yourself comfortable: the interesting part comes now."

Elaine knew that Smith was a maniac for the truth, and that he would never claim that a courgette was a courgette if he hadn't first done all the tests possible and imaginable; so she sank into her dark honey coloured leather armchair, preparing to listen to the rest of the story, and wondering with increasing insistence what the hell she had to do with that incredible story.

4

Elaine looked absent-mindedly at her watch, as soon as the two men had left.

Ten past seven p.m.! Damn, she had to hurry! That evening she had been invited to dinner by Linda, and she knew from experience that in her house at eight o'clock one sat down to eat. She liked to arrive a little early and converse with her friend, so as not to give the impression that she was only there for dinner, so she almost ran to her room, but as she was taking off her blouse, the image of a plane in flight materialised in her mind, and a slight tremor ran through her from head to toe. She was angry with herself for accepting that strange assignment, before she even knew it involved at least one flight to Italy. Not that she was unhappy about travelling to Tuscany, quite the contrary; she would finally be able to see her father's land, breathe the air he had breathed in his youth... and then Tuscany was one of the most popular destinations for travellers from all over the world.

But it's not the trip to Italy. It's the plane. That damn thing that makes a hellish racket and terrifies me. What if I go by ship? That's good, so you'll arrive next year...Come on, try to be brave! Yeah, that's easy to say...

They had just finished eating when Minnie, like a perfect ruffian, jumped onto Elaine's neck and started purring, rubbing her muzzle against her open palm.

"The red potato pie was really delicious... Linda, you are a perfect cook."

"Don't flatter me, Elaine! Otherwise I'll end up believing it and opening a restaurant!"

"You could do it just fine, believe me...sometimes people eat in really awful places! I'll help you wash the dishes now," Elaine said as she stood up.

"Just sit where you are. I'll wash them in the morning. In fact, let's go to the living room on the couch, so you can finish telling me about that gentleman...what did you say his name was?"

"Zimbaldi. Professor Francesco Zimbaldi."

They sat in the living room and Elaine lit a cigarette.

"You still haven't told me what he's like...is he handsome?" Linda asked, handing her a crystal ashtray. Elaine laughed. The idea of considering Zimbaldi from that point of view had not even crossed her mind.

"I don't think you'd find him to your taste... he's a bit of a... he's very strange, that is."

Linda shrugged her shoulders, "My poor Eddie was strange too... yet I spent the best years of my life with him. Come on, finish your story! Or have you decided to leave me on tenterhooks?"

"There is little to add to what I have already told you. It seems that this Roberto Birindelli was never interested in the Middle Ages... at least until 1998. Then, after a bad accident in which he hit his head, strange things started happening to him, such as seeing people dressed in medieval clothes, or witnessing scenes from that period. A real puzzle. Sometimes all this also causes him physical ailments, but we've talked a little about that."

"But you...what does this have to do with you?"

"I am assigned to check the reliability of this whole thing. Professor Smith brought me some material collected by Zimbaldi; he has already examined it, and now I will have to read it. Then I'm going to Italy to talk to this gentleman," Elaine said with a sigh.

"What, Elaine! To Italy? By plane? But you're afraid to fly!" exclaimed Linda, spreading her arms wide in a ridiculous imitation of a plane.
'Of course I'm afraid! A bloody fear! It doesn't matter if you remind me... if you knew what a time I'm having! As soon as I close my eyes, I see planes everywhere!"
"But it's wonderful! In Italy! I was once in Paris, and I assure you the experience was unforgettable... Europe is so full of charm and history..."
An idea suddenly flashed through Elaine's brain.
"Linda! Why don't you come too?"
"Me? But you're crazy! How do you come up with such ideas?"
"I'm sorry, what's wrong?" repeated Elaine insistently, "You're retired, and I don't think you have such pressing commitments that you can't take a holiday. After all, it would only be five or six days!"
"What about the cats? How can I leave the cats alone for a week?"
"Yeah, I forgot about the cats... I mean, Linda, there are also pet boarding houses."
"My kitties in a boarding house? Never!" Linda shrieked as she got up from the sofa; then she resumed more calmly, "No, look, it's just not possible... I'm so sorry, because seeing Italy has always been my dream... but I can't, really. And that's my last word."

5

It was eight o'clock in the morning, and a light mist made the image of the planes that could be seen looking through the large window of J. F. Kennedy soft and delicate.
The trolleys with luggage moved silently from plane to plane, while the refuelling vehicles stood beside the aircraft.
Elaine and Linda were sitting comfortably, waiting for the call of their flight to Rome and sipping a coffee that had a distinct after-taste of chicory.

Barely five days had passed since Elaine had taken the job, and very soon she would be boarding the plane that would take her to Italy.
She was trembling with fear. Her handbag was full of tranquillisers and motion sickness pills: she had literally emptied a pharmacy amidst the smiles and veiled surprise of the clerk who served her.
She looked at Linda, who was peacefully stretched out on the comfortable armchair, and felt a tinge of envy; Elaine struggled to keep her composure, but without any appreciable results. On the contrary, the more time passed, the more her anguish grew.
She knew that Linda was thinking about Minnie and the other two cats. They had found an alternative solution to the animal boarding house. Elaine had remembered that she had an acquaintance who never went out, not even to go shopping; she had the shop assistants bring everything home. She had spoken to Linda about it, and together they had asked her if she would be able to look after the three animals for a week. The farewell between Linda and the cats had been heartbreaking. She had held out

as long as she could, but then, as soon as she and Elaine got into the taxi that would take her to the airport, she burst into unstoppable tears. After five or six miles the taxi driver, a big black man the size of a wardrobe, had politely asked if she was feeling ill, and Elaine had told him about the cats. Incredibly, he had been moved too; and surprisingly Elaine had finished the journey amidst Linda's cries and the good black giant's frequent loud nose blowing.

The call for their flight finally came: Elaine jumped up, took Linda by the arm and said, in a voice too loud that immediately betrayed her fear, "Let's go! This is our flight!"
As soon as she uttered the word "flight" her legs gave out. "Damn these shoes... I almost fell on the ground!" she exclaimed contritely, trying in vain to escape Linda's wary glances.
With all the formalities done, they entered the moving tunnel to their plane.
As soon as they entered the interior of the aircraft, Elaine felt a little reassured: it was much larger than she had expected, and soft classical music made the surroundings pleasant and restful. Their seat was in first class, and Elaine found herself seated near the window. When the stewardesses had finished seating all the passengers, the onboard loudspeakers began spewing out all the safety information; but Elaine only felt a little better when she realised that right next to her was the emergency exit.
The plane began to move slowly, and entered the runway. Then it stopped, and lay still for three or four minutes. To Elaine those moments seemed like an eternity. Linda's voice shook her.

"This is it. Now the pilot will turn on the turbines and we will take off...how do you feel?"
"I thought worse. It's so big in here..."
The plane started up. Slowly at first, then faster and faster, as the noise became deafening. Elaine closed her eyes, and felt herself pressed against the backrest. When she opened them again, she looked out the window and saw New York as she had never seen it before in her life. The plane was turning right over the island of Manhattan, and she could easily make out the Empire, the Twin Towers, the Brooklyn Bridge and the UN building; in the bay, the Statue of Liberty seemed to be waving at her.

She had read Zimbaldi's material and found it extremely interesting. She had come to the conclusion that this man, this Roberto Birindelli, if he had been a fraud, would have had to have been incredibly good, and above all he would have had to have had a background on the subject that many of the leading luminaries of medieval history did not possess. She couldn't find anything anachronistic in the writings: everything fit together perfectly, everything was described meticulously and precisely. It seemed as if the man was living two lives, one real, in the present, and another of pure fantasy, in the Middle Ages that did not belong to him. But it was a disconcerting fantasy.
Elaine had tried to reduce it to a more practical dimension, as Smith certainly had, but she had failed. There were so many stories from that Birindelli, as the collection covered the whole of 1999 and the first two months of 2000.
She was beginning to find this Zimbaldi, who had even had the bright idea of recording Birindelli with a

small digital camera, for the use of which he was probably squandering more than half a salary buying videotapes.

Yes, undoubtedly Zimbaldi had a way of working that she liked. Everything written on those sheets was pure reporting, without the addition of the slightest comment.

The stories were written in a strictly scientific manner, and in chronological order: at the top of the sheet appeared the date, then the place, then began Birindelli's description, usually preceded by a couple of questions that served to introduce the subject.

The day after Zimbaldi's departure, Professor Smith had returned to Elaine and they had talked for almost two hours.

Smith had confessed to Elaine that he had been puzzled above all by the fact that Birindelli, during his visions, never spoke of castles, armourers, damsels or anything else easily related to the Middle Ages, but only of the quiet daily life of a very normal family living and working in a village in the heart of Tuscany.

He also told her that he did not know the exact location: he knew it could not be very far from Livorno, and he hoped to be able to pinpoint the exact place and finally find some tangible evidence.

"What year would one place this story in?" had asked Elaine.

"It hasn't been figured out. I'm pretty sure the whole thing dates from around the year one thousand, but I don't know exactly," Smith had replied, shaking his head.

"There's one thing that's not very clear to me... this Francesco Zimbaldi... what does he want to do? I mean, even assuming Birindelli lives some kind of reincarnation or something, what are his plans?"

"From what I can gather, he hopes to write and publish a book on the subject in question... he would certainly achieve success and notoriety. Then there is another aspect of the matter to consider." Smith enthused, "If all this were true, do you realise that we would have an individual in constant contact with the Middle Ages? Think of all the things we ignore on the subject!"

"Easy, professor, easy! Don't get ahead of yourself!" said Elaine laughing, "You have to recognise that this whole thing has absurdity in it. Put yourself in my shoes... at least wait until I've spoken to this Birindelli."

"I already have," Smith had said. "In fact, along with all the material I brought you, you will also find an interview I did with the subject three months ago, during my trip to Italy. Read it carefully. I am sure you will find it interesting."

"Milk or coffee?" The voice of the hostess who was bringing the breakfasts distracted her from her thoughts.

"Coffee, thank you. Look, could I also have a glass of water?"

"Certainly. And you ma'am?" the stewardess continued, addressing Linda.

"All that's possible to have. I'm so hungry, I could eat the pilots and the whole crew."

The stewardess nodded smiling, and quickly filled the table in front of Linda with every good thing: Coffee, milk, rusks, butter and various jams, a glass of orange juice and even some bacon with an egg omelette. And of course the maple juice carton.

"This is travelling first class!" exclaimed Linda, immediately attacking the omelette.

They landed at Fiumicino at ten o'clock Italian time; Elaine thought not without a hint of nostalgia that it was four o'clock in the morning in America, and if she had been home she would still have had at least three more hours to sleep.
The connection that was to take them to Pisa, where they would find Zimbaldi waiting for them, was scheduled for twelve o'clock, so they decided to spend those two hours visiting the many shops inside the airport.

Chapter Three

Tuscany, Italy.

She is mine. I feel her everywhere. She is all around me. She understands me, she fulfils all my desires. But not love. I will have to take care of that. Beautiful countryside, incomparable sunsets, incomparable food. But no love yet. I must go back, I must. I can't stay here inside this strange amber cloud. There's no point. I must live. I must love. And then maybe die. It doesn't matter. But first I must find love.

1

It was seven o'clock on the last Sunday at the end of March, and Roberto Birindelli was making the final preparations for a cycling trip with three of his friends from the Ecologists' Club.

The previous evening he had overhauled his mountain bike, noting with satisfaction that it was the picture of efficiency.

In the accident two years earlier, his old bicycle had been completely destroyed, so he had had to buy a new one.

The insurance company had paid him twelve million for his injuries, since the accident was entirely the fault of the investor, so Roberto had the choice of the best on the market. After seeing and trying out different models of bicycles, he had opted for a mountain bike made in Japan, completely built in light alloy and equipped with an eighteen speed Shimano gearbox. He had paid a hefty sum for it, but it was certainly worth it.

Two days earlier he had received a visit from Francesco Zimbaldi accompanied by the history expert assigned to study it in depth, one Elaine Giuliani.

He knew she was American, but had been happy to discover that she spoke and understood Italian well, because even though he knew English, certain feelings he experienced during visions (he now called them that) he was afraid he could not express them in a language other than his own. Besides, Giuliani was good-looking, which didn't hurt at all.

The plan for the day was to drive inland from Livorno towards Siena; the main roads would be deliberately avoided thanks to the guidance of a true expert, a certain Antonio Mariani, who knew the area like the back of his hand.

It was decided to stop at a trattoria where the speciality was wild boar stew served with slices of polenta, so they would not have to carry rucksacks with provisions.

That morning Zimbaldi would join the group, together with Elaine and Linda; naturally, they would travel by car, so they arranged to meet at the trattoria.

In Roberto's life, Marta was no longer there.

She had left him, she said, because she could no longer cope with the absurd situation of living with a visionary, someone who one moment was there with her and the next was telling stories of medieval life and describing her beautiful green eyes that were brown. She was fed up, and five months earlier she had given him the ultimatum: "Either you stop this nonsense or I leave you," she had said imperatively and dramatically.

Roberto had done everything he could to make her understand that it was not up to him, and that sometimes he found himself saying or doing things he would never have thought or done spontaneously. For a month or so Roberto had been very careful, carefully avoiding any reference to the matter, and always finding an excuse to absent himself when he realised something was wrong.

The bomb had gone off while they were making love: he had called her Celeste, and without a word she had dressed and left.

He had never seen her again, not even by chance.

At first he had suffered, cried, calling himself stupid for not reacting enough. At first. Then, after a few days, Roberto had stopped suffering. He had questioned himself, and had hastily concluded that perhaps he did not love Marta as much as he thought.

But the truth was another, much more disturbing.

It was time to tell himself the truth.

Somehow Riccardo had managed to enter inside Roberto, and when he manifested himself, he managed to convey his feelings to him. It was now Roberto who loved Celeste as much as Riccardo, he felt he also owed Raterio respect and gratitude for teaching him the blacksmith's trade, along with many other things; he was sure that if they had given him the right stone and a scythe he would have rounded it to perfection.

At least two or three times a week he became Riccardo, and in those moments he had learnt to sit and wait for the visions: they were passages of daily life. It was the grape harvest in September, the olives picked in November, the winter evenings spent with Celeste and her family in front of the fireplace, weaving baskets or drinking wine in merriment.

All this did not manifest itself chronologically or logically, but rather casually: one day he would watch enchanted summer sunsets, and the next day he would find himself immersed in a freezing winter morning, with the cold getting into his bones and forcing him to cover himself more than necessary.

The visions were not mere, evanescent tricks of the mind, but were akin to real cinema films: everything flashed before his eyes, three-dimensional figures and places, and he smelled and heard sounds so intense they took his breath away.

He understood very little of what was said, but he could almost always grasp the meaning of the sentences, even if they were pronounced in a strange language that must have been a mixture of Latin and the local dialect, Vernacular. And in any case, Latin had very little to do with what he had studied at school.

He had never seen Riccardo's face, for the latter's eyes were his time defeating cameras.

2

After three hours pedalling along dusty, pothole filled roads, fatigue was beginning to set in. Having left Livorno at eight o'clock on the dot, after two kilometres on the state road they immediately plunged into the countryside, skirting long rows of vines and brushing past farmers engaged in the seasonal pruning of olive trees.
Occasionally they were joined by some joke like 'O bischeri! Or where are you four going in such a hurry?'
But they paid no attention, just smiled and pedalled on.
It was about an hour that Antonio Mariani continued to say he knew those roads like the back of his hand, and was encouraging the other three: 'Come on! The trattoria is just behind that bump!' or 'Ovvia! Now we're nearly there... around that bend!'
But there was no sign of the trattoria.
Roberto was the last of the four, since the accident he had had two years earlier had left him with a small but annoying hematoma on the back of his left thigh, which often caused him annoying cramps. But he endured stoically, and pedalled hard so as not to get too far behind his companions.

At twelve twenty, they finally reached the trattoria.
It was a large renovated farmhouse used as an agritourism, frequented mainly by foreign tourists, mostly English and German.
The building, not very tall, stood on the top of a rise surrounded by a pine forest; a narrow tree lined avenue about a kilometre long led to the provincial road, but what was most striking was the marvellous

old terracotta roof, which, silhouetted against the blue sky, gave the place an appearance of immense peace.

A small pool to the right of the building was the delight of three little girls as blonde as wheat, who had a great time bathing each other and splashing everyone who unluckily passed by.

In the barn, not far away, there were rooms for up to eleven people.

There were not many cars in the car park, and Roberto immediately recognised Francesco Zimbaldi's Renault.

The four got off their bikes, and burst out laughing as soon as one of them exclaimed:

'Here we are. The four wild geese!"

Then they headed towards the entrance, where Professor Zimbaldi and the two women were waiting for them comfortably seated on wicker chairs, sipping an aperitif.

"At last! We had given up hope by now... but where have you been?" Said Francesco getting up and walking towards them, followed by the two women.

"Ask him." replied Roberto pointing at Antonio, "In my opinion that gentleman wanted to show us around a little longer than planned!"

Having made the necessary introductions, the seven people entered the dining room and sat down. Roberto was particularly happy that his seat was directly opposite Elaine's.

The meal was excellent and plentiful; jokes and laughter were wasted, but Linda, who did not understand a single word of Italian, did not participate much in that atmosphere of serene cheerfulness.

In return she ate like a regiment of bersaglieri and drank an entire bottle of Chianti. When the coffee arrived, she entered powerfully into the social life of the group, and astonished the diners by singing almost the entire Elvis repertoire and improvising an improbable drum kit with spoons and glasses. Then she rested her elbows on the table, took her face in her hands, sighed, called Minnie twice and fell fast asleep.

Antonio and the other two friends decided to leave immediately for Livorno; Roberto would return in the car with Zimbaldi and the two women. He had already put the bicycle in the boot of the Renault, not without difficulty, tying the upper hatch with a rope secured to the bumper. To prevent the rear wheel of the bicycle from touching the rear window, he had inserted cardboard all around the wheel.

"What do you say we take a walk to digest what's in our stomachs?" said Roberto thinking back on the excellent but hearty meal.
"You go ahead... I'll stay here with Linda," Zimbaldi said, pointing to the woman who had meanwhile been carried to a wicker couch, and who was now soundly snoring.
Roberto and Elaine walked towards the pine forest, along a lane strewn with daisies and violets. When they reached the forest, they saw that the path continued through the pines; they walked along it until the trees came to an end, and a large green valley opened up before them, which a small stream cut exactly into two equal parts.

"Now I understand why Tuscany is such a popular destination," Elaine said in Italian, enjoying the landscape.

"Beautiful, isn't it?"

"Gorgeous. And then you eat very well."

"Yes. Linda especially seems to have enjoyed it a lot." laughed Roberto.

"She's always like that. She says she eats too much, that she should lose weight, and then she manages to gobble up everything in front of her..."

Roberto looked at Elaine, but did not see Elaine. It was Celeste who was smiling at him and walking beside him. She kept talking about Linda, and Roberto could understand perfectly everything she was saying. He was amazed. It was the first time something like this had happened.

"It's... it's happening," Roberto whispered, fearful that the vision would disappear.

Elaine stopped and turned towards him, looking at him intensely. "You mean that right now you have...you see something?"

"Yes. I see Celeste...she has taken your place."

"How is she dressed?" said Elaine as her heartbeats were accelerating dramatically.

"No... no dress. Just the face. The eyes... the colour of your eyes are identical to Celeste's. There, now she's disappeared. It's you again."

Over the previous two days, Elaine had had several conversations with Roberto, and each time the thing that had impressed her most was his simplicity. He told the facts that had happened to him in a lucid and straight forward manner, never getting carried away by situations. She had become convinced that he was not a braggart, and she seriously thought that this whole story deserved proper investigation.

But she was not prepared for such a situation.
They walked back the way they came, in silence, while cold shivers ran unceasingly down Elaine's back.

That night Roberto had a hard time getting to sleep. The vision of Elaine's body with Celeste's face had disturbed him, and he tossed and turned in bed wondering why. Then he finally fell asleep. And he dreamed.
The sun was setting behind the hills in the distance, and coloured the whole valley in front of them with a mellow, intense amber; there they were again, he and Elaine, just where the pine forest ends: in front of them the usual green valley opened up, and there was the usual stream, only a little larger; but on the opposite side of the stream stood a village.
It was deserted and silent. Not a bird song, not a breath of wind.
Roberto approached slowly, trying not to make noise so as not to disturb that peace.
When he got close to the stream, he discovered to his horror that instead of water, blood was flowing.
He turned to Elaine, and saw that the woman was crying.
Her face was rapidly decaying, until only two empty eye sockets remained, looking at him in horror.

3

Linda liked Italy. It was full of monuments, history, traditions; the locals (that's what she called the Italians) were friendly and kind. Everything was on a human scale, even if compared to America the facilities left something to be desired.

She missed her cats, and yearned to hug them again, cuddle them, hear them purr and play with them. Sometimes she cried, but always at night, when she was alone. She found Francesco Zimbaldi a fascinating person, and more than once during her five day stay, she had confessed to Elaine that she wouldn't mind having a fling with him.

Francesco had taken the two women to visit Florence, Siena and Pisa, and, of course, Livorno.

When Linda had seen the Piazza dei Miracoli in Pisa she had remained still, motionless, enraptured to the point of not speaking, standing in the middle of the square, heedless of the group of Japanese tourists who had surrounded her.

Then, after exclaiming an *Oh my God* of convenience, she had collapsed in Zimbaldi's arms, who, suddenly finding himself carrying that unexpected weight, had struggled hard not to let her fall.

Roberto had not had many opportunities to accompany them on their sightseeing forays, as school took up most of his day, but the few times he had done so he had been happy to be with Elaine, towards whom he was beginning to feel more than just affection.

With her he could talk about any subject: she was intelligent, and above all she could listen, a rather rare quality in a woman. Elaine often tried to bring up the subject of why she had come to Italy, but she felt that Roberto was more and more reluctant to talk about it.

They had even gone to dinner alone, on the port of Livorno, and Roberto had wanted Elaine to taste the cacciucco; it was in that restaurant that they had begun to get to know each other and call each other by name; they had talked all evening like good friends, and when they had returned they had exchanged a chaste kiss on the cheek.

Zimbaldi and Elaine had tried to analyse the strange dream Roberto had had, and had come to the conclusion that it had nothing to do with his visions.

"It was merely the unloading of your mind from all the tensions accumulated during this last period," Zimbaldi had ruled with authority.

But Roberto felt that this was not the case: there was an underlying truth in that dream, a message that he did not understand, but that was somehow linked to what he was seeing in the past.

Chapter Four

New York, USA.

I would like to fly. But I cannot, I can't. I have to stay in here. Inside the amber. It protects me, it gives me soft light. I cannot do anything but love. Because it is the only thing still worth living for. I am now master of time. I don't care about space. I have my mind. It is enough for me. I don't want anything else, and even if I wanted it, I couldn't have it. Not now.

1

It had already been eight days since they returned to America, but Elaine and Linda still had Tuscany in their eyes. It had entered them to the point where they found themselves every evening talking about the experience and looking at the pictures Linda had taken. They had almost all come out crooked, and when they came across the picture of the Tower of Pisa perfectly straight, they burst out laughing.
Linda had found her cats in perfect health, in fact, Minnie had even gained weight.
They cuddled her a lot, and this time even the lady who had looked after the little beasts was a litt e moved.

Elaine had had the opportunity to speak with Dr Scott, and had told him the facts about the various meetings she had had with Roberto Birindelli. She had also prepared a detailed report of her days in Italy with the subject, but had not yet felt able to hand it over to the professor. She felt that many details were still missing in that report, indeed, many fundamental things, and what she had put down on paper was only the small part that had emerged from the iceberg.

She was beginning to think that this whole thing could not have happened by chance, just because a primary school teacher had hit his head in a car accident. No, there was definitely more to it than that.

She had read and reread all of Roberto's stories and watched Zimbaldi's videotapes; she had made copies of them, which now lay there on her desk.

Roberto often telephoned her and kept her informed of developments; sometimes he telephoned her even though nothing had happened, and when this happened, Elaine felt a shiver go down her spine. He would also send her many photographs of Tuscany using e-mail; huge files that would open in half a day: but she was waiting in front of the computer the whole time.

She didn't know how Professor Zimbaldi intended to proceed with Roberto, but she was certain that he would never give him away to the press or to a group of scientists anxious to study his brain, and this partly reassured her.

Elaine felt strange.

She had only once experienced being with Roberto when he had visions, and the fear she felt at first had soon turned into endless sadness. She continually tried to read inside herself, to try to understand the

reason for this melancholy, but she could not. She just couldn't.
Until what should never have happened, happened.

It was the second Thursday in April, and the clear morning presaged a warm and sunny day. Elaine decided to ditch work and go for a walk in Central Park.
She put on her tracksuit and red basketball shoes and left the house.
She walked down the pavement, past the Metropolitan Museum and onto the path that would take her to the lake. She stopped at a street seller and bought a bag of peanuts for the squirrels.
There were not many people there, not least because it was nine o'clock in the morning on a working Thursday, so she felt as if she were immersed in unspoilt nature. She thought back to the beautiful Tuscany countryside, and considered that in any case Central Park was also a beautiful place, an invigorating treat for New Yorkers.
She saw a squirrel standing at the foot of a tree and threw a peanut, then looked at it. She loved the frantic work of his little paws as they freed the fruit from its shell.
She arrived at the lake followed by three or four squirrels who claimed their share. The most enterprising among them came within a few centimetres of her feet, and began to look at her, making little leaps and waving his soft brown tail.
"You must be the pushiest of the bunch. And that's fine. You've earned it," Elaine said, tossing him a peanut.
Roberto. How strange, she couldn't get it out of her head. No man had ever had that effect on her. She

was sure that if they dated, something could have been born....

But he lives in Italy... and you in America. It takes nine hours by plane to meet! Wow! Talk about bad luck. You finally think you have found the right man and where do you find him? On the other side of the Atlantic Ocean...

She continued thinking about Roberto and playing with the little animals for a good half hour; she had almost finished the peanuts when a cloud covered the sun and the light took on a delicate amber colour that coloured everything around her: then her attention was drawn to a man sitting on a bench not far from her. Strange, she had not noticed him until then.

His back was turned, and from the short tunic he wore, he seemed to belong to a religious set or something similar.

The man was hunched over himself and moving rhythmically, as if....

God, please don't let him be masturbating!

There was no one else around them, and the squirrels were gone.

Elaine had often heard about the maniacs who frequented Central Park, looking for lonely women or even children to molest, so she began to be afraid.

To get back on the path she had to walk past the bench where that strange individual was sitting.

She plucked up her courage, got up and walked slowly, without making the slightest noise, always keeping an eye on the man who quietly continued to do his work.

By now she was so close that if she had stretched out her arm she would surely have touched him, and

she could distinctly see the man's hairy legs, and also the back of his left hand with a deep scar. The man turned his head and stared at her. He was not masturbating.
In his right hand he held a stone, and in his other hand a scythe. But it did not look like he had evil intentions.
He was just rolling it.
Elaine stood petrified, as the man said something to her in a strange language she did not understand; she tried to speak without succeeding, so she took a couple of steps back, turned and started running. She stopped only when it seemed to her that her heart was about to burst.

As soon as she got home she tried to phone Roberto, already knowing that he would not answer; he was surely at school at that time. As she promised herself to try calling him again in the early afternoon, she was already forming Smith's number.
"Hello?" the voice of Professor Smith made her breathe a sigh of relief.
"Professor, it's Elaine. I need to speak to you." she said breathlessly.
"Alright... but why are you out of breath? Goodness, have you been running?"
"Yes... when can we meet?" she asked.
"So..." Elaine knew Smith had put on his glasses and was consulting his diary "Three o'clock in the afternoon?"
"Good. Are you coming over?"
"Alright. See you there."
She sank into her armchair, lit a cigarette, closed her eyes and tried to think.

She had just seen a man who probably did not exist. In fact, he definitely did not exist. But how was that possible? She had not had any accident, she had not hit her head like Roberto, let alone been in Tuscany. She was in New York. She began to speak out loud, as she always did when analysing some extremely complex case. "So...this man does not exist. But I saw him. He was real, and if I had wanted to I could have touched him. I could even smell him. And then he spoke...what did he say? It's useless, I don't remember... he was rolling an old scythe. Right in the middle of Central Park. Easy, Elaine, easy... write it all down. And consult Zimbaldi's notes."
Elaine opened her desk drawer and picked up the packet of reports marked Birindelli. After five minutes, she was again reading the descriptions given by Roberto during his visions, and everything matched perfectly, from the colour of his hair to the scar on the back of his left hand. But she already knew. She just wanted confirmation.
The man in the park was Raterio.

2

Smith removed his glasses and stared at her for a long time "Elaine, I don't know what to say."

"Neither do I. You may be thinking now that I'm a visionary, and that I've gotten carried away by this situation.... God willing!"

"I don't know, Elaine, I don't know... I really don't know what to think... although I'm inclined to believe that this is all a figment of your over-excited imagination. How many times have you read Zimbaldi's report?"

"Several times. I know it almost all by heart by now." replied Elaine, then continued, "And I've seen the tapes at least a dozen times too. I too thought it might be a figment of my imagination...but my God, it was all so real, so...so present!"

"It would be a normal thing if your mind had played this nasty trick on you. I said 'would be' because I know you well, and I find it hard to believe that somehow you have lost control...on the other hand, I see no other solution. Try to keep calm, and if anything like this happens to you again, phone me immediately," Smith said, getting up and walking towards the door. "One more thing... at the end of April I have to go to Italy to receive an award. I was wondering if you would like to come with me. I know very well that you are puzzled by my proposal, because maybe you think the best solution is to unplug... at least for a while. But sometimes the direct impact with the problem works wonders."

"In Italy?" said Elaine pleasantly surprised, "And where?"

"In Rome. But of course I'm going to Tuscany afterwards. If you come too, I'll let Zimbaldi know, so

he can book you a hotel... in fact, let's do that. I only have to stay one day in Rome. If I can get away from my commitments here in New York we could spend a fortnight in Tuscany...what do you say?"
Elaine barely suppressed the urge to scream and hug Smith.
"I don't know...I'll have to see the schedule. Now off the top of my head I can't say."
"Alright, alright, I admit I was a bit hasty...I'll tell you what: I'll phone you in a couple of days and confirm the exact departure date, so you can give me your availability," Smith concluded.
"Alright. I'm supposed to go to New Jersey tomorrow night. Just give me a call there. Goodbye Professor, I'll talk to you on Saturday."
As soon as Smith had closed the door behind her, Elaine clenched her fists, and kept repeating, "Yes! Yes!" as she headed for the bathroom.

3

The next day, Elaine returned to Vineland to spend the weekend there, dragging Linda along with her, under the pretext of finally showing her home in New Jersey that she had told her so much about.
But it was, indeed, an excuse; the truth was that Elaine was afraid.
Professor Scott had tried to reassure her, trying to convince her that a mind saturated with strange information can play such tricks, but it had not been enough.
Other times she had found herself in particularly stressful situations, but she had always come out on top, and never had her brain or her body done anything she hadn't wanted to.
But one must also consider that everyone can say something like that until it doesn't happen... there is always the first time. Take heart Elaine. You won't go crazy over this. Or maybe you've already gone crazy and didn't realise it.

They arrived at the Vineland house at seven-thirty p.m., after a very quiet drive of about two and a half hours. There was still plenty of light, and they could tell it had been a sunny and warm day. Elaine hoped it would be nice weather the next day as well, because she wanted to take Linda to see the surroundings of the city. She operated the remote control that opened the electric gate of the garage and went inside, immediately turning off the engine.
They unloaded the car and, after Elaine had cleared the house alarm, entered through the back door, which led them into the large kitchen.

"Oh, my goodness! But it's beautiful!" exclaimed Linda as she helped Elaine open the windows, "I wonder how you can live in New York having such a place!"

"The work, dear, the work. You know very well. Besides, anyway, I like New York too. I must say that I have found the ideal combination: work in the greatest city in the world and rest in the quietest city in America."

Linda freed her cats, who began to roam around the house sniffing everything within sniffing distance; the quietest was Minnie, who quickly found a comfortable home by curling up in an old rocking chair Old America style.

Elaine had brought the supplies she needed just for that evening; the next morning she would go to Bobby's shop to buy what she needed, then stop by Charlie and Rita's Muzzarelli's Farm to buy the red potatoes Linda was so fond of.

They sliced a large Tuscany salami that they had brought back from Italy two months earlier in defiance of their country's customs laws, and put on the table a bottle of Vernaccia di San Gimignano that Elaine had paid an arm and a leg for in a New York shop: thirty-two dollars for less than a litre of wine, but it was definitely worth it.

If for no other reason than to think back to those wonderful days in Tuscany.

The taste of salami immediately awakened in them the memory of the quaint agriturismo where they had eaten many of the delicacies offered by the excellent cuisine, and a bit of nostalgia assailed the two women.

Elaine was shaken by the thought that the following week, if she had wanted to, she could have gone back there with Roberto: she was homesick for him, and couldn't wait to see him again.

They ate with appetite, and not to contradict themselves, Linda took out half a salami and several sandwiches; even the cats seemed to appreciate the little bits their mistress gave them. After two hours, the bottle of wine was finished, and the two women found nothing better to do than to go to sleep.

Early the next morning, the phone rang. Elaine was already up, and was preparing breakfast.

"Hello?"

"Good morning Elaine, it's Smith. How are you feeling? Have you calmed down a bit?" asked Smith on the other end of the phone.

"Good morning Professor. Yes, I am better. Nothing new has happened to me. I too believe it was a bad joke due to stress," replied Elaine.

"Listen Elaine, I have to be in Rome next Friday at ten o'clock in the morning...I've checked the flights from New York, and ideally I'd like to leave at six thirty on Thursday. If you can confirm your availability I'll have my secretary get the tickets."

"All right. I wanted to know how long we'll be in Italy, though," Elaine said.

"It's up to you. I've kept about twenty days free...and as you know I don't have any family commitments," Smith replied, once again reaffirming his membership of the bachelor club, "anyway we can come back any time you want."

"Twenty days is fine. This time I'd like to see Rome as well," said Elaine.

"Goodness, I hadn't thought of that. Just think, I was so sure you'd come that I've already phoned Zimbaldi... he's going to pick us up in Rome by car right after the award ceremony, so we can be in Livorno in the evening." said Smith sorry he'd rushed things.

"It doesn't matter, Professor. If we come away from Tuscany two days before the date of our return flight, we could visit Rome." said Elaine, pleased with that idea.

'It can be done. Good, then I'll get in touch on Tuesday for the final details... ah, Zimbaldi told me to ask you if the hotel from last time is ok for accommodation."

"Definitely. Tell him I'll phone him." confirmed Elaine, then paused briefly, "Has Roberto been notified?"

"I haven't called him, but I think Zimbaldi has... anyway, if you want I'll phone him," Smith offered.

"No, never mind, I'll take care of it. Goodbye Professor, I'll talk to you next week."

Elaine lowered the handset just as Linda, followed by Minnie, was entering the room.

"Good morning Elaine...how well did you sleep? I didn't even hear a car..." said Linda yawning.

"Good morning sleepy head! Come on, let's hurry up with breakfast, I'll take you to see the sights of the city!" said Elaine as cheerful as ever.

Linda looked at her surprised, "What happened to you? Did you spend the night with Brad Pitt?"

4

Charlie was serving some customers when Elaine and Linda stopped the car near his farm on the state road.

Muzzarelli's Farm had been the official vegetable supplier to the Giuliani family for more than twenty years, and never would Elaine have dreamed of buying a produce in Vineland that wasn't grown on that farm.

The owners, Charlie and Rita, both of Italian descent, grew vegetables and potatoes on an immense expanse of land. They also employed many Mexican workers, some of them involved in the preparation and packaging of the sweet potatoes exported all over the world.

Elaine and Linda had already been to Bobby's to buy some food supplies, and now they were waiting for their turn to bring home some sweet potatoes.

Elaine greeted Charlie "Hi Charlie, how are you? This is Linda, a good friend of mine from Boston who has her house in New York right next to mine....

And where's Rita?"

"She's at home making breakfast. We're running late this morning because we've had quite a few clients... if you want I'll call her," Charlie replied in his characteristic baritone voice.

'No, never mind... I'd like some sweet potatoes...' said Elaine.

And right there, as Linda watched Charlie preparing the potatoes, it happened again.

Elaine was admiring different varieties of apples displayed in the wooden crates, when she felt the overwhelming urge to grab one.

She picked up the apple and was feeling it for firmness when it fell to the ground.

The apple tumbled under the counter near Linda's feet, and Elaine bent down to pick it up. As she was getting up she was struck by a severe dizziness, and would certainly have fallen if a man's strong arm had not supported her. She looked up and saw a young man in his early twenties looking at her, smiling. One of the man's hands was clutching her arm so that she would not fall, and the other was outstretched towards the apple, as if he wanted to catch her.

Elaine noticed with growing terror that the man had a short tunic tied around his waist with a rope, and she clearly heard a word escape his lips, "Celeste..."

She closed her eyes tightly, straining not to scream, and when she finally decided to open them again she discovered with relief that it was Linda who was holding her up.

"Elaine, what are you doing?"

"Nothing... I just slipped..." replied Elaine to her friend's concerned request.

Chapter Five

Running without a moment's pause. I don't know, or maybe so. But now I want to go back in time. I can do it. I can travel through the dark, not giving a damn about science. I hate science. It keeps me alive, but I hate it. I wish it didn't exist. Or I wish I could create it. As I like. As I wish. Then I wouldn't be here. I would be resting.

1

The flames were devouring yet another oak log that Raterio had placed inside the large stone fireplace, but it seemed to Celeste and her mother that that fire gave off no heat, so cold was the evening. It was snowing like it had not done in years, and the three of them, not seeing Riccardo return, were beginning to think the worst.

Even though the distance to the forest where Riccardo had gone to get more firewood was short, the pitfalls of winter could be many: ice to slip on, a large branch laden with snow that breaks, starving wolves that gather in packs and attack.

It was already the middle of March, but such a cold day had not yet occurred that year.

The winter had been rather mild, but with this latest tailspin it seemed to want to make up for lost time. Many trees were already full of buds, and Raterio knew very well that with such a frost they would not bear fruit this year.

The north wind blew hard, and the trees in the forest made a terrible noise; lightning and thunder followed one another without ceasing; the room was constantly illuminated by the flashes of the many thunderbolts that ripped through the sky.

Raterio was afraid that it was only the prelude to something catastrophic; if it continued to snow with that intensity, perhaps the roof of the house, although partly new, would not hold the weight, and would collapse on their heads. He thought that he had not been very far-sighted: he might have planted a central pole to prop up the roof: although it would not have looked good, it could have guaranteed the safety of the whole structure.

Two years earlier, he and Riccardo had done quite a job, renovating and reinforcing the worn out parts of the roof, but nothing suggested such weather, nor could Raterio remember such weather.

The door suddenly opened, and Riccardo quickly entered, closing it immediately behind him. He remained still, standing in front of the door, looking at Celeste strangely, who immediately thought something had happened to him.

"Riccardo! What has happened?" asked Celeste in an anxious voice, without getting an immediate answer.

"Speak... don't keep us anxious!" now Celeste was almost about to cry.

"He spoke to me..." said Riccardo in a hushed voice.

"He spoke to you? And who spoke to you?" asked Raterio.

"God. God spoke to me."

It had been two years since Riccardo had arrived in that family, and now Celeste was six months pregnant. She didn't have much of a belly yet, but she could feel that new life constantly moving inside her, and this brought him immense joy.

Her mother had never been as caring as she was at that time: she avoided heavy work for Celeste, and always advised her to be careful not to fall.

Raterio was happy too, and looked forward to holding his grandson in his arms. Or the granddaughter, who knows.

The midwife, who hadn't attended a birth for two years, came by at least twice a day to check on the condition of the mother-to-be; she was already forty-two years old, and she knew she didn't have long to live, being of advanced age. Perhaps it would have been the last child she would have patted behind her back to make it cry also because, apart from Celeste, there were no other pregnant women in the village.

Raterio's was a Christian family, although there were no churches in the village to go to for prayers. In fact, there was still a church, but it was almost completely ruined, and there hadn't been any priests in the village since his father's time. On the other hand, once every two months a friar, usually Candido, would come by to bring the word of the Lord to the inhabitants of that community.

Riccardo was also religious: Edoardo, his old friend and teacher, had taught him the basics of the Christian faith, telling him about all the martyrs who had sacrificed themselves in the past to hold high the name of God.

Edoardo had especially advised him not to give in to temptations, and to be very careful, because the devil was devious, and could change his appearance as he pleased.

Riccardo had been very impressed by these words, and had once asked him:
"But is he really so terrible?"
"More than we men can imagine."
"And how do I recognise him?"
"Don't worry," Edoardo had replied, "from the moment you doubt something or someone, God will come, and he will help you understand, speaking within you and showing you the right way."
And now Riccardo had indeed heard God speaking within him.

2

Celeste came out of the house to empty the bed pots, and the landscape before her left her breathless: it snowed almost every year, but she had never seen anything like it in her life.

After three or four steps, she found herself knee deep in snow and realised that she could not go any further; she emptied the contents of the bed pots onto the white blanket, which melted to the surface on contact with the still warm liquid.

Suddenly, a mass of snow broke away from the roof of the house and fell close to her, causing her to wince. Celeste looked up and saw her father busy clearing the roof of the snow that had accumulated during the night: he had climbed up a tree a few metres from the house, and with a long wooden pole, he was making the snow fall to the ground.

It had stopped snowing recently, but the temperature was still very low, and the bitter cold made all kinds of work difficult: it was one of those days to spend in front of the fire drinking warm wine.

There had been no particular damage caused by the storm; the roof, despite Raterio's doubts, had held up well to the weight of the excess snow, although during the night a couple of sinister creaking noises had made them fear the worst.

Celeste thought of Riccardo: what had happened to her man the night before had shocked her, and they had talked about it most of the night, until the eyes of the two had closed from tiredness.

God had spoken to Riccardo.

At first she had thought it was a joke, because she knew Riccardo well and knew that he loved practical jokes: the previous year he had skilfully attached a few bunches of cherries to an olive tree, shouting at the miracle, and wondering what oil would come out of such olives. They had been laughing for days, thinking back to the astonished faces of the villagers who had come to see this strange phenomenon.

But she knew it was no joke this time: she had realised it almost immediately by looking at Riccardo's face. He appeared transfigured, and his eyes opened wider than necessary to reveal that something had greatly upset him.

He had told him that God did not speak normally, as they did, but directly inside his head, and although the wind had blown hard the previous evening and the noise was unbearable, he could hear it clearly, and had not missed a single word.

"What did he say to you?" asked Celeste, resting her head on his chest.

"So many things. Above all, he asked me questions. About you, about your family. About our life in this village. He also knew how we met, and he told me that he saw us that time we went to Liburna," replied Riccardo, holding her tightly.

"God was watching us?" exclaimed Celeste incredulously, thinking back with shame to when they had made love by the sea.

"So he told me."

"But how do you know he is God? Did you ask him? How can you be sure it's not the Devil?" had asked Celeste.

"I... I feel it. When he talks to me, he is good, patient. He told me to call him Roberto, but I know he wants that because I must not take his name in vain."

Now Celeste was afraid of God. Afraid that he would take her man away from her and ask him to dedicate his life to him. At that moment she decided that if this came to pass she would fight with all her strength and all the means at her disposal to keep Riccardo by her side. She would have fought even against God.

3

The next day in the early afternoon, Riccardo went into the forest.

The weather was good: the sun had already returned in the morning, and the cold had abated, so that the snow accumulated on the branches of the trees had begun to melt, and, dripping from above, formed deep holes in the blanket below.

He and Raterio had shoveled the snow around the house, but the road to the forest was still hardly passable, and Riccardo proceeded slowly, changing the still pristine landscape step by step.

He arrived at the beginning of the forest, and breathed a sigh of relief when he saw that there was less snow under the trees than in the fields; much of it was deposited on the branches, and glistening in the March sun.

He went to the same place where God had spoken to him two days before; the silence was absolute. Not a breath of wind, not a song of birds.

Riccardo thought of Liburna and how beautiful it must be with the snow. He imagined the sea as an immense white swaying board, and flocks of white birds crouched above.

He saw a large stone sticking out of the ground, and after clearing it of snow he sat down upon it: and the waiting began.

But time passed, and nothing happened.

Although he had been careful to wrap his sandals well, the rags were now soaked with water, and the cold on his feet had become almost unbearable.

To beguile the time, he cut a dry twig from a tree and began to draw marks on the white blanket of snow, and as he was drawing nonsense he suddenly

realised his presumption: how could he think that God was at his disposal? How could he be so foolish as to believe that he would only manifest himself because he, Riccardo, wanted him to?
He threw the sprig away in annoyance, and got up, determined to return home.

The light was beginning to fall, and the cold was more intense; Riccardo was sure that at home he would find the fireplace burning and the two women preparing dinner. Raterio was not there that day, and he would not be there the next, as he had gone to a village to do an urgent job: it took courage to walk through that snow, but Raterio had courage to spare. Surely Riccardo would have been useful to him, but now that Celeste was seven months pregnant, he preferred to leave him at home with her and her mother.
"You'll be more useful at home," Raterio had told him in a good natured tone. "There are two scythes to be sharpened, and there's the handle to be put on that knife on the mantelpiece. Then you provide the firewood and the chickens." Riccardo knew very well that Raterio trusted him blindly, and that it was useless for him to tell him what he should or should not do: but his was a way of feeling like the master and reminding him that he was the one who had welcomed him into his home; therefore, Riccardo accepted his way of doing things benevolently.
His thoughts went to Celeste: she had realised she was pregnant in November, during the olive harvest. She had sung, shouted, danced, such was the happiness of giving him a child.
That very evening they had decided on a name. If it was a girl, she would be called Matilde, Edoardo if it

was a boy. Celeste did not like the name Edoardo very much, but had kept quiet, as she was aware of the history between Riccardo and his old friend.

The harvest had lasted eleven days, but Riccardo's time had flown by, and he had done the hardest work almost without noticing it: he was always cheerful, and talking to him was a pleasure, so much so that the villagers often came to visit him, especially in the evenings, for a laugh.

He resumed his journey home, disappointed that he had not been able to listen to God.

Tomorrow I will return. Tomorrow I am sure he will speak to me.

That night Riccardo could not sleep. Strange, unknown objects appeared in his mind, like four-wheeled carts that travelled without being pulled by horses, and huge birds that flew through the skies without flapping their wings, leaving behind a wake like the boats on the Liburna sea.

4

The next morning Celeste's mother opened her eyes, awoken by the glow coming from the window; she went to see, and realised that the sun was already high. She wondered how she had been able to sleep so long, slipped on a pair of leather sandals and went to open the door to the chickens, shivering at the contact of the snow that entered the sandals.

When she arrived at the hen house she noticed that the chickens were already outside; the heat of the day before had melted a great deal of snow, and the beasts were scratching around in the places where the earth was re-surfacing and the mud was playing havoc. Evidently Riccardo had already got up and sent the poultry out. She was about to re-enter the house when her attention was drawn to a dark spot in the snow, not far from her.

From her position she could not tell what it was, also because she could not see very well, so she cautiously approached until she saw a slowly moving tail. She thought it was a fox, but then looked closer and discovered it was a dog. The poor beast, probably exhausted by cold and hunger, turned its head towards her and yelped faintly.

She returned to the house, and found Celeste intent on stoking the fire. She told her what had happened, and together they ran out to help the beast; they almost collided with Riccardo, who, returning from the woods, had picked up the dog and was bringing it into the house.

"Did he speak to you this morning?" asked Celeste, putting some bread in a bowl.

"Yes. He spoke to me," replied Riccardo, gently depositing the beast in front of the burning fireplace.

A pang pierced Celeste. "And what... what did it tell you?"

Celeste's mother came out with the bucket, under the guise of fetching water from the stream; she had actually realised that the conversation was becoming a private affair between her daughter and Riccardo, and being a very discreet woman she thought it best to leave them alone.

"I asked him what he wants me to do," replied Riccardo.

"Ah..." said Celeste, adding water to the bowl to soften the bread.

"You are afraid. Don't deny it, I can feel it. You are afraid." Suddenly, Riccardo looked into her eyes. "You are afraid that he can take me away from you. You've been acting strange for two days."

Celeste was taken aback by Riccardo's words, but then regained courage, "Well... I am afraid, yes! I'm afraid he'll ask you to dedicate your life to him..."

"I realised that." said Riccardo, holding her close and kissing her cheek where a small tear was falling.

"Take it easy. He told me not to worry. That's not what he wants from me... he just wants to talk. To know how we live, what are our dreams, our hopes. He tells me so many things, makes me see with my mind the world of our children, and I assure you that you couldn't even imagine it. Sometimes I don't understand him, so he explains things to me patiently, as one would with a child. He still wants me to call him Roberto, and I slowly start to get used to it. He told me that our children's houses will be very big, and each of them could accommodate all the inhabitants of this village, and that people will travel on wagons that run on iron pieces and inside big

birds that fly. I even dreamed about them, you know?"
A sudden yelp accompanied Riccardo's last words. Celeste placed the bowl in front of the beast's snout, which began to eat greedily. Then she looked at Riccardo who was watching the dog, threw her arms around his neck and wept tears of joy.

Chapter Six

Tuscany, Italy.

I am starting to get used to it. But I know I don't have much time left. I am about to go home. I will miss this enchanted place. I can do whatever I want. Here I am, God. I can create, paint pictures with landscapes and people that never existed. I have only one colour, amber. But that is enough for me. And then sometimes I hear music. Classical music by Vivaldi, Mozart and Chopin. And when I don't want to hear it any more I just think it fades away, and the music fades away. Because here I am, God.

1

"But really, have you noticed or not that we are here too? If you want to give us some of your attention, we can even talk in four. But then, what will you have so important to say to each other, I just can't understand..."
The speaker was Professor Smith, and the sentence was addressed to Elaine and Roberto, who were sitting in front of him and Zimbaldi, but who seemed to be light years away from them.

When Elaine had arrived in Livorno six days earlier, Roberto had greeted her with the long kiss they had both been waiting for, in front of two bewildered history luminaries who had never imagined such a thing.

Elaine had not gone to the hotel Zimbaldi had booked for her; she had instead settled in Roberto's house, and was spending a few days with him that were as wonderful as they were unexpected.

They had decided, by mutual agreement, to stay together for the twenty days that Elaine would be in Italy; then they would make a decision.

And things were going decidedly well so far. Elaine rediscovered the thrill of sex, and perhaps to make up for lost time, the two of them made love very often, sometimes even three times a day.

How different Roberto was from her ex-husband! Never hurried, always considerate and helpful. He was ready at any time to fulfil her every little wish.

In the morning Roberto went to school, to his children, as he said, but the afternoon was all for her, and together they were discovering a world of fulfilling happiness from which they thought they were now excluded.

Roberto hoped that Elaine would want to settle in Tuscany; they would perhaps look for a bigger house, and she would surely find work, if only as a translator; he was unaware that Elaine was well off, and he was afraid that her future doubts were dictated by economic insecurity.

They were now seated in the usual restaurant where they had eaten a few months earlier, and music wafted through the air, the notes of Vivaldi's Four Seasons.

"Sorry," said Elaine, smiling, "we were forgetting you."

"Eh, blissful youth!" replied Zimbaldi, sipping an excellent white wine from Monte Carlo.

"By the way, your friend, that Linda, is she all right?"

"She sends her regards, Professor Zimbaldi." replied Elaine, then continued, alluding "I'm afraid she has broken a heart, across the ocean..."

Zimbaldi gave a little cough, then quickly changed the subject, "This wine is great...I shall have to remember the brand," he said, taking the bottle and looking at it.

"We haven't had a chance to talk about it yet," Smith said in English, turning to Roberto, "but I'd be curious to know something about your visions."

"I understand very well, but I ask for your patience... a lot of other things have happened recently, and I promise you that I will soon make you aware of the latest developments in this story, and, believe me, they are quite interesting." This sentence spoken by Roberto in somewhat limp English managed to arouse the curiosity of everyone, including Elaine.

"All right, all right, we have plenty of time," Zimbaldi repeated, "Now let's finish enjoying this delicious dinner."

Elaine was puzzled. She had never spoken to Roberto about this topic since she had arrived in Italy, because she felt it was only right that he should be the first to address it.

But now that she knew about the important developments, she wondered why she had not yet spoken to him about it. Did he want to be sure he would be believed?

No, that couldn't be the reason.

And then did you behave better? Did you make him aware of your apparitions? No, you did not. Then shut up.

Elaine had said nothing to Smith about her last incident either. She was more and more convinced that it was fatigue, not least because, thinking back on the incident, there was at least one thing that supported her hypothesis.
When the image of the man at Charlie's farm had appeared, she had distinctly seen that the short robe he wore was tied at the waist with a rope.
As soon as she returned to New York, she had immediately gone to check whether this detail appeared in Smith's reports, but had found no trace of it. She had believed the man might be Riccardo, but had no proof. But she knew that Roberto's description of the latter was sketchy: it was more a matter of sensations than anything else, but as far as the description of his physical appearance and manner of dress was concerned, the elements that appeared in Zimbaldi's writings were few and rather vague. And it was a logical thing, since Roberto in those particular moments saw with Riccardo's eyes, and therefore, unless he stood in front of a mirror, he could not know his face either.
"Tomorrow is Saturday, and it is my cay off at school. I want to take you to visit Lucca," Roberto whispered in Elaine's ear.

2

Lucca was truly one of the most beautiful cities Elaine had ever seen in her life.

She and Roberto had strolled for a long time on the walls; then they had gone to browse through the streets of the centre, walking slowly and stopping in front of all the shop windows; Elaine had seen a strange cake in a bakery and had bought it. She had then discovered that it was 'buccellato', a kind of sweet bread with raisins that was a local speciality.

They were sitting at an outdoor table in an ice-cream parlour in Piazza dell'Anfiteatro, and Roberto was laughing like mad because Elaine had had the waitress bring her ice-cream in a bowl, and was now spreading it on the open buccellato like a sandwich.

"Damn! But can you eat it all?" asked Roberto laughing.

"Of course I can! And don't hope to help me finish it, because I'm not giving you a single crumb," replied Elaine as she continued to spread the ice cream.

"Alright, alright...but try not to overdo it, otherwise you'll ruin your dinner...tonight I'm taking you to eat in Montecarlo."

"Montecarlo? Isn't that in France?" asked Elaine surprised.

"No, not that...Montecarlo di Lucca." replied Roberto laughing, "The village where they make the wine we drank last night at dinner. It's near here...it's about fifteen kilometres away."

"And how are we going there? You don't have a car...is there a train?" asked Elaine, taking a mighty bite of her unique maxi-sandwich.

"We'll take a taxi, that way we'll be quicker... then, since tomorrow is Sunday and I'm free from my school commitments, we'll sleep in Montecarlo."
"But..." tried to retort Elaine.
Roberto brought his finger in front of his mouth, "Shut up. Don't say a word. You'll see you'll like it."
"Yes, but tomorrow we were supposed to go with Smith to a museum," said Elaine.
"You can go some other time. Besides, on a Sunday there are people everywhere, let alone in a museum! No, I'll keep you all to myself tomorrow,' concluded Roberto in a tone that admitted no reply.
And while Roberto was talking, it happened again, right there in Lucca, in Piazza dell'Anfiteatro.

Elaine was transformed. Not suddenly, like the other times, but slowly, like a computer reconstruction: her face took on Celeste's features, and her elegant pink blouse changed into a white, foot length dress: a light amber veil materialised above her head, covering her hair.
And her eyes changed colour.
Roberto stood open-mouthed, continuing to look at her: before him, fused into a single icon, the two women he loved more than anything else in the world were eating a buccellato filled with ice cream.
When those green eyes rested on him, he immediately realised that something was wrong: they stared at him in surprise, as if they saw something different from what they were looking at. And that was indeed the case.
Elaine continued to stare in amazement: standing before her was the same man who had held her up at Charlie's farm. She no longer had any doubts. It was Riccardo. And she could also see, through the

perforated wrought-iron table, the rope around his waist.

They stood like that, looking at each other for about ten seconds, without deciding to speak.

"I...you are..." whispered Elaine under her breath, perhaps afraid to break that sort of spell.

"So are you. We are them. Each in the other's eyes. You don't have to be afraid. Whatever happens, you don't have to be afraid. I understand one thing: they are good, they don't want to hurt us,' Roberto said.

"But why us? Please help me understand, otherwise I'll go crazy."

"Try to keep calm. I know it's difficult...let's keep talking. If they want something, we will soon realise," said Roberto.

A sudden light flashed in Elaine's eyes.

"I want to make love to you." she said getting up and placing the buccellato on the table.

"So do I. Let's find a tree to lie in the shade." Roberto replied as he got up in turn and wrapped his arms around her waist.

They kissed. It was a long and intense kiss, a prelude to something more satisfying, which drew a few comments and a couple of applauses from a group of tourists who were visiting the square.

The enchantment broke, and Roberto and Elaine walked away, leaving the buccellato at the mercy of a cheeky little sparrow who immediately began to peck at it frantically.

3

Zimbaldi's flat was on the second floor of one of Livorno's most luxurious areas; it had cost him a fortune, and to buy it he had almost entirely drained his share of the inheritance his parents had left him.
The study was furnished soberly, without frills or useless knick knacks: a large bookcase covered almost the entire wall opposite the front door, and a chestnut desk served well to house a small laptop computer and a 1930's style lamp that was a true antique.
The room was not very large, but two large windows made the room bright and warm; the windows overlooked the sea, and even though they were at a considerable distance, during sea storms the windblown spray could reach the glass.
Zimbaldi was very attached to that study, where he spent most of his free time, dividing it between reading and playing the guitar, but every time he picked up the instrument a lump rose in his throat, and he started thinking about Luca again, and how everything would have changed if he had been there with him.

It was just after ten o'clock in the evening, and the lamp on the desk diffused an amber light that illuminated the whole room; Zimbaldi was sitting at the desk, while Roberto, Elaine and Smith were entering the room.
They sat down on chairs that completed the study furniture, and all four of them looked at each other for a long time without speaking. Eventually, Smith decided to introduce the subject, in English of course.

"Well, here we are. We are curious about the latest developments in this matter,' he said, turning to Roberto.

"Excuse me, Professor Smith, but I would prefer to speak in Italian... I feel more comfortable," apologised Roberto.

Zimbaldi quickly settled the matter. "Don't worry. I have my tape recorder here. I'll turn it on, and then I'll get the writings in English to Professor Smith. In the meantime I will translate the most important things to him verbally."

"Then let's begin," Roberto said, waiting until the tape recorder was switched on.

"I have already told you that some new facts have occurred that I think are important, and when you know what they are, I am sure you will feel the same way." The atmosphere was tense, and the tension palpable.

"By now you all know that strange, unexplained facts have also happened to Elaine, which no doubt relate to this affair." Elaine and Zimbaldi nodded.

"We will talk about that too, but the main reason I wanted us all to be together is another." Roberto paused briefly, then continued.

"I can now say with certainty that this whole thing is not just limited to visions, but has become something more...how shall I put it? More complete, that is."

The sound of a burglar alarm siren from the street momentarily eased the tension.

"Riccardo speaks to me. He knows me. He knows who I am. And through me, he begins to see what the future will be like."

The siren suddenly ceased. Now only Zimbaldi's whispering voice could be heard, translating Roberto Birindelli's last words to Smith.

"And that's not all," Roberto continued, "Riccardo asks me questions. And I answer him. I tell him about our life, about what the world will be like a thousand years after his time."

"But you..." Elaine interrupted him, "can you talk to him whenever you want?"

"No. Our contacts now are frequent, but casual. I'm sure there's a trigger, but I haven't been able to identify it."

"And what did you tell him about us?" asked Zimbaldi momentarily suspending the English translation.

"Everything. Or almost everything, what I thought was most important for him to know. I told him about our homes, our big cities. I tried to make him understand what cars are, and I told him we can fly."

"And he understands these things?" asked Zimbaldi again.

"I think so, but I'm not sure. The questions he asks me are intelligent, but he has not yet accepted the idea that I am a man. He thinks God is speaking to him."

Smith, after Zimbaldi's last translation, whispered something in his ear.

"The professor says this is normal: a simple mind that lived a thousand years ago...that finds itself hearing voices speaking to it...it is normal for it to think of the voice as God's. But how can you understand what it says, since it does not speak your language?" translated Zimbaldi.

"I don't know about that. But it happens automatically, as if we were two people sharing the same brain. Of course his vocabulary of words is very limited. When I told him about the car, I had to use simple vocabulary, describing it as a wagon with wheels, without horses, and so on... in short, it's as if I were talking to a savage." said Roberto.

"Can he also see the future in the same way you can see the past?" asked Elaine, increasingly impressed by the tale.

"I don't know, but I don't think so... I think Riccardo can only talk to me. And my visions are different too. Lately they are veiled, elusive, encased in a strange amber light... there, just like that," replied Roberto, pointing to the lamp on the desk. 'Exactly like the first apparitions I had. There, that's the latest news."

"Sounds like important news to me," Zimbaldi said, switching off the tape recorder.

"Until now," resumed Elaine, "we have been trying to discover the cause of these strange events, without ever asking a question that in my opinion is very important... especially now that I too, as you well know, have been personally involved."

The three paid full attention.

"What is the point of all this? I mean, couldn't what is happening be related to a very specific purpose? Couldn't we simply be the actors in a play written by someone whose existence we ignore? A higher entity that is using us for a purpose or end that we ignore? Please don't look at me like I'm a crazy person... I simply made a hypothesis. And anyway, if what I said seems bizarre to you, try to think of everything that has happened to Roberto for the past two years...and to me in the last few days. I think all avenues should be explored to try to discover the causes and effects of this affair."

Zimbaldi finished translating Elaine's speech to Smith, then the latter took the floor, in English of course.

"This hypothesis is very interesting, even if it seems a tad over the top to me... on the other hand, thinking well about the whole affair, the oddities followed one another in a disturbing crescendo, and I wouldn't be surprised if Elaine with her suppositions was on the right track."

Zimbaldi was about to translate what Smith had said into Italian, but Roberto stopped him by nodding to tell him he understood. He then smiled at Elaine.

"Mah, to me this theory seems the most absurd part of the whole thing...what would be the purpose of whoever would be doing this to us? No, let's try to keep our feet on the ground..."

"Feet on the ground?" snapped Elaine getting up, "Feet on the ground! Look, maybe this has become so normal for you that you don't even notice it anymore, but do you realise that for two years you have been seeing, hearing, smelling the life of a family that lived almost a thousand years ago?"

"Calm down..." said Roberto, taking her arm to sit her down.

"I will not calm down, no!" Elaine freed herself from his grip with a tug "Now this is about me too, do you understand? I don't want to end my days in an asylum, seeing men in skirts and holding scythes appear before me!"

"All right, all right, let's try to deal with this calmly..." said Zimbaldi, motioning Elaine to sit down "That's certainly not the way we're going to resolve the situation. Let's try to examine even the smallest details. I am sure that there is at least one detail that unites almost all the events..." then he turned to Roberto in Italian "Am I talking too fast? If you want I can do the translation for you."

"No, go ahead... if I don't understand something I'll stop you," replied Roberto, implicitly congratulating himself on the excellent level he had reached in his study of English.

"Well, as I was saying there is one thing that puzzles me. It may well be that I've made a mistake, and that what I'm about to tell you is just a coincidence, but at the point we're at, you have to hang on to every little foothold. Amber. The amber light, which appears in almost all of Roberto's visions."

"The amber?" exclaimed Smith, "I hadn't thought of that... but it's true. That is certainly an important detail..." Smith's voice was excited.

Elaine intervened, "I wouldn't swear to it, but that man I saw in Central Park was also surrounded by... yes, I remember now! Everything around me was amber in colour, as a cloud covered the sun... and it was at that very moment that I saw him!"

"What do you think it could mean?" asked Roberto intrigued by this new theory.

"I don't know," replied Smith. "All I know is that thanks to Zimbaldi here, we now have something we can actually work on."

Chapter Seven

They have discovered amber.... that means they are getting closer. But it's not time yet. It's like shaking something in your hand and then opening it and realising there's nothing there. Nothing real, nothing true. Maybe someone is listening to me. Or maybe not. In the end I don't care. I am still God. Here. And I have to go back down there. I have to, otherwise it will never end.

1

It was long past that very cold March that had whitened the whole valley, and the June sun was beating down hard that day; the air was rendered unbreathable by the dreadful sultriness that seemed to come straight out of the earth, distorting reality with a continuous gelatinous movement immersed in a monotonous chirping of cicadas.
Riccardo, seated in the shade of a large tree, was enjoying a proper rest after mowing a field of clover; he thought that he would soon go to the stream to wash himself, and he would finally be able to cool off in those cool, immaculate waters.
A rabbit peeped through the grass, sniffing the air with quick movements of its little head.

When word had spread in the village that Riccardo was talking to God, not a day went by in the early days without someone asking him about various things: someone wanted to know how the harvest would go, someone wanted to know when the cow would give birth, someone wanted to know which prayer he should recite before falling asleep.

Riccardo replied to everyone that God did not speak of these things with him: he spoke of something else, much more important things, but that the time had not yet come to reveal them. After a while, people got tired of hearing him answer in this way, and some even began to claim that he was crazy. But Riccardo didn't care. He knew it was true.

Probably God wants me to see the future because humanity is behind the times, and someone has to put things right. Maybe I will not be that man, but in due time God will point me to the right person to reveal to him all that I know.

He got up not without difficulty and walked slowly towards the stream, thinking he would like to share those moments with Celeste. But the midwife had put her to rest, advising her to lie down and not to move: the baby could be born at any moment, and it did not look like an easy pregnancy; therefore, it was not the case to take unnecessary risks.

As soon as he reached the stream, he took off his sandals and stepped barefoot into the water: the coolness brought him immediate relief, evoking in Riccardo sweet memories of the sea of Liburna and golden beaches of sand so fine as to be almost impalpable.

He washed himself well, with care, then put his sandals back on and headed home: he would soon be resting his face on that round bump that he now loved like nothing else in the world.

When he came within a hundred steps of the house, he saw a figure standing in front of the door, fidgeting: he immediately realised that it was Raterio, who was scrambling to get his attention. Riccardo jumped the path and started running directly across the fields, avoiding obstacles with great leaps.

When he reached his destination he noticed that Raterio was crying.
"What...what has happened?" asked Riccardo, feeling bad.
Raterio did not answer, and continued to cry louder. Riccardo entered the house, and with his heart in his throat he crossed the kitchen and crossed the threshold of the room, from where he heard heart rending screams.
Celeste's mother, the midwife and another woman were standing around his bed, where his love lay motionless.
Her belly was gone, and next to her was the baby wrapped in a white sheet.
They were both dead.
Riccardo fell to his knees in disbelief; he tried to speak, but could not articulate any sound. He began to cry, and crawled towards the bed. He took Celeste's hand and kissed it, first slowly, then more and more frantically, shouting and cursing God's name until Raterio dragged him away and carried him into the kitchen, forcing him to sit on a bench beside the table.
Riccardo's shoulders were shaking, and with his hands he beat his chest and punched the table hard. Then he got up and walked out of the house, followed at some distance by Raterio.
Riccardo raised his hands to the sky.

"God! Where are you? Answer me!" he shouted with all the breath in his body, "Am I not your pupil? How can I care what you tell me about the future if I have no future? How can you talk about my children's children? Celeste is dead! Dead, do you understand? And the child is dead too! Is that my future? A life without Celeste? I don't want it!" Riccardo slumped to the ground, shaken by sobs and weeping.

At that moment a cloud darkened the sun, and everything was tinged with amber, while a strange but very sweet music spread through the valley; Riccardo wiped his eyes and thought that the Lord was there with him, and would hear him.

"God, please hear me... Celeste is dead, and the child she was carrying is also dead... please do something. You can do everything. You are God."

2

It was long past that very cold March that had whitened the whole valley, and the June sun was beating down hard that day; the air was rendered unbreathable by the dreadful sultriness that seemed to come straight out of the earth, distorting reality with a continuous gelatinous movement immersed in a monotonous chirping of cicadas.

Riccardo, seated in the shade of a large tree, was enjoying a proper rest after mowing a field of clover; he thought that he would soon go to the stream to wash himself, and he would finally be able to cool off in those cool, immaculate waters.

A rabbit peeped through the grass, sniffing the air with quick movements of its little head.

When word had spread in the village that Riccardo was talking to God, not a day went by in the early days without someone asking him about various things: someone wanted to know how the harvest would go, someone wanted to know when the cow would give birth, someone wanted to know which prayer he should recite before falling asleep.

Riccardo replied to everyone that God did not speak of these things with him: he spoke of something else, much more important things, but that the time had not yet come to reveal them. After a while, people got tired of hearing him answer in this way, and some even began to claim that he was crazy. But Riccardo didn't care. He knew it was true.

Probably God wants me to see the future because humanity is behind the times, and someone has to put things right. Maybe I will not be that man, but in due time God will point me to the right person to reveal to him all that I know.

He got up not without difficulty and walked slowly towards the stream, thinking he would like to share those moments with Celeste. But the midwife had put her to rest, advising her to lie down and not to move: the baby could be born at any moment, and it did not look like an easy pregnancy; therefore, it was not the case to take unnecessary risks.

As soon as he reached the stream, he took off his sandals and stepped barefoot into the water: the coolness brought him immediate relief, evoking in Riccardo sweet memories of the sea of Liburna and golden beaches of sand so fine as to be almost impalpable.

He washed himself well, with care, then put his sandals back on and headed home: he would soon be resting his face on that round bump that he now loved like nothing else in the world.

When he came within a hundred steps of the house, he saw a figure standing in front of the door, fidgeting: he immediately realised that it was Raterio, who was scrambling to get his attention. Riccardo jumped the path and ran straight across the fields, avoiding obstacles with great leaps.

"It is born!" said Raterio in irrepressible joy "It is a boy and he is well...and Celeste is also well. She is waiting for you. Run!"

With three leaps, Riccardo reached the room, where he found Celeste's mother, the midwife and another woman talking to each other and smiling.

Lying on the bed was his love, smiling at him and holding a completely amber-coloured child in his arms. Riccardo

began to cry tears of joy, thinking back to the time when Celeste and her son lay lifeless on that same bed.
He did not know when it had happened, but he knew it had happened.

Thank you God. Thank you for having granted me. Now I know that I am truly the chosen one.

Chapter Eight

Amber. Amber. Amber. I can't take it anymore. It has to stop. I'm one step away. I know it's not up to me, even if I continue to be God here. But somehow it must end.

1

Elaine had decided to settle permanently in Italy, and it was now four months since that April when Roberto had proposed to her to live together with him, marry in September and maybe even have children in time.

She had returned to America, but only to settle her affairs for good. She had sold her house in New York to an advertising graphic designer who was quite famous in his circles, but she had left the stocks and bonds unchanged; she had simply diverted the proceeds of these investments to a bank in Livorno, where she had opened a current account in her and Roberto's name, who was pleasantly surprised to learn of Elaine's financial assets.

Linda and her cats were hurt by the sudden and final departure of their best friend; Elaine had tried to sweeten the pill by saying that she would return to New York often, but Linda would not listen to reason. She had cried and fasted the day before her departure, the same day and the day after. Then she had decided that was enough, and to console herself she had started eating more than before.

Roberto and Elaine had bought a large house in the countryside inland from Livorno, four kilometres from the sea; although they had been able to live comfortably, they had both decided to continue working.

Elaine had contacted the company that had taken over her father's shoe factory, and now she and Roberto were taking the necessary steps to set up a company that would export Italian raw materials for shoes overseas.

The house was spectacular, surrounded by greenery, with a large park full of ancient trees that guaranteed coolness even on the sunniest days.

They had paid nine hundred million Italian lire for it, slightly less than what they had earned from selling the house in New York. On the other hand, Elaine had not wanted to know about parting with the house in New Jersey, and had promised to go there with Roberto to spend the following Christmas.

The contacts between Roberto and Riccardo still continued, in fact they were much more frequent than before: it was not uncommon for them to spend whole days talking to each other.

Roberto had gone through the traumatising experience of Celeste's death with Riccardo, and had been shocked by the irrational end of the affair. He had spoken about it with Elaine, who had written to Professor Smith via e-mail, and had also contacted Zimbaldi; they had agreed to get the four of them together to discuss the matter. Smith replied, again by e-mail, that he had important revelations to make, and that this latest episode fully confermed his hypothesis; Zimbaldi, for his part, had abandoned his research on Roberto two months ago, because it did not seem right to him to enter into the intimacy of the newly formed family.

Professors Smith and Zimbaldi had decided to stay for a couple of days, and would arrive that very afternoon: the house was very large, and there was no shortage of rooms.

Elaine had had no further appearances. She was constantly following the development of events, but had not been directly involved since that day in Lucca.

She was worried about Roberto: in the moments when he was in contact with the past, Elaine preferred to distance herself, because she found it unbearable to see her man sitting with his eyes closed, silent and completely absent from everything around him; she had tried to talk to him in those moments of catalepsy, but Roberto had not even opened his eyes.

However, there was one thing that bothered her more than Roberto's behaviour, albeit unconscious: amber.

It had become a recurring thing. It was now the most frequent colour in their lives; even the new house was painted externally in this colour.

Elaine had spoken to Roberto about it, but he did not seem to give too much importance to this fact; yet it was an undeniable fact that every day their eyes collided with something that should have been another colour, and instead was amber.

Lighter, darker, exploiting the possible shades: but still amber it was.

The doorbell rang, and Elaine operated the remote control that opened the gate to the park; after a few moments, the unmistakable sound of the wheels on the gravel of the driveway leading to the house, heralded the arrival of a car.

Early the next morning, Elaine got up to prepare breakfast for her guests; she went down the stairs and walked towards the kitchen, but noticed that the front door of the house was open. She went to check, and sitting on the veranda found Professor Smith busy reading some papers that filled the wicker table in front of him in an untidy manner.

"Good morning, Professor," greeted Elaine, surprised to find him up at such an hour. She knew his flight had arrived the previous evening, and wondered how on earth he had managed to absorb the inconveniences of the time difference so well, which to her would have ruined at least the entire next day.

"Good morning Elaine..." said Smith taking off his glasses and placing them on the table, "As you can see I have dispelled the legend that makes us Americans chronic sleepers."

"How come you were up so early? Was the bed uncomfortable?" asked Elaine thoughtfully.

"No, in fact... it's soft just the way I like it," replied Smith, "Could we have coffee?"

"Certainly. I'll go make it right away... American?"

"Can you do that?" asked Smith, who had never got used to the strong, sharp taste of Italian coffee.

"Yes, I brought the electric coffee machine with me from New York," replied Elaine as she re-entered the house.

Smith smiled. Elaine was an exceptional woman, and he had always admired her, because she was able to deal with the situations in front of her in a logical and rational way, always finding the solution to any problem. He had worked with her for many years, and he could not remember ever seeing her give up when faced with something that did not convince her: she was capable of spending entire days doing research and did not stop until she was convinced she had got to the bottom of it.

But this time it was different. This time there was no solution, and he knew it.

All he needed to do was to make a check to have his suspicions definitively confirmed.

He put his glasses back on and started reading his notes again.

2

"By now I am almost certain that what I have just told you corresponds to the reality we are experiencing at the moment; all that remains is this last test to be done, and then we will have mathematical certainty. God forbid I'm wrong."

Elaine and Roberto looked at each other in dismay, as Zimbaldi eagerly flipped through Smith's notes: he could not believe that the solution to the enigma that had nagged him for two years was the one Professor Smith had just announced.

Yet the reasoning that Smith had brought to support his hypothesis was irrefutable, and his previous observations had now convinced him that it could only be so.

Elaine was partly right. There was someone pulling the strings of their lives. Commanding them, making them act according to a pattern, whether rational or irrational.

All that remained was to carry out this test. The litmus test.

Smith turned to Elaine, "Do you have anything amber that you think should be a different colour?"

Elaine thought for a moment, "Yes, several things... I don't know, for example, even that flower in the vase behind her. In my opinion they should be purple."

"Look... in my opinion this is a crazy theory." said Roberto taking the vase containing the flower in question and placing it on the table "Yes, it's true, some things do match, but from here to think we're all being manipulated..."

"Listen to me, Roberto" Elaine interrupted him with gentle firmness, "we have no other recourse. If you want this to end, let's do as the professor says..."

"That's exactly the point. I'm not sure I want it to end. I've grown fond of Riccardo, of his family... and then he needs me. He thinks I am God! I can't say goodbye and thank you for everything... it wouldn't make sense, you know?" repeated Roberto, raising his voice a little too much.

Smith intervened: 'I don't know if you have thought about it, Mr Birindelli, but that man, that Riccardo, has the right to live a normal life...he can't go on talking to a supposed God forever and have things changed that he doesn't like. But the most important thing is that we are now sure that someone is listening and watching us. And based on what we say or do, he changes or leaves reality unchanged. To his liking. The thing about Celeste. Celeste, who is, let's say, 'resurrected' together with her child. You know very well, Roberto, who did this: it was the one who controls us. He saw what had happened and did not like it; therefore, he changed what had already been."

Zimbaldi tried to convince him, "What does it cost you to try? From what the professor said, it will be a very simple thing."

"I don't know, I have a feeling... if what he said is true, this superior being, or whatever he is, has absolute control over our lives! What if what we're about to do he doesn't like and destroys us? Have you thought about that, professor?" said Roberto, turning to Smith.

'I have thought about it. In fact, to tell you the truth, I haven't thought about anything else for a while now.

But that's not necessarily the case... it may well be that he only has control over events concerning Riccardo and his family. After all, he has never changed our lives: at least not in a way that we

would notice. Still, it is a risk we have to take. Besides, we are rational men. That we reason, that we are not intimidated by a flower or any other amber-coloured thing. No, we have to try, if only for the sake of science,' Smith replied in a tone so solemn that it admitted no reply.
Roberto nodded, and all four of them arranged themselves around the table, concentrating on the pale amber flower.

After a few minutes, Professor Smith had confirmation of his theories: the flower disappeared, and all that remained was a useless stem to which only a small green leaf was attached.

Chapter Nine

By now things are going badly. Or good. I can't understand it. I'm starting to be a little less like God. And I am as tired as I have never been in my life. But do I have a life? Now all I have to do is look the other way. Then I will decide. For I am still powerful.

1

Raterio was thinking back to the events of the previous day. His grandson had been born. A beautiful child, there was no doubt about it. But he was the colour of honey. And this he did not understand. He didn't understand it at all. He had never seen a man or a woman of that colour.

Once they had told him that in a neighbouring village a lamb had been born with two heads, and he and some friends had set out to see the strange phenomenon with their own eyes; but when they arrived two days later, they had seen nothing at all, because the lamb in question had died, and the owner had burnt it, convinced by the other villagers that it was the work of the Devil.

Of course this whole thing was strange... he wondered who Riccardo really was.

Perhaps an angel? Or an envoy of the Lord? Riccardo talking to God, his child the colour of amber... Riccardo learning immediately and effortlessly all that it had taken him years and years to learn, Riccardo always helpful, obedient, kind.

He resumed ploughing the field behind the house with renewed vigour, thinking about the sowing he would have to do soon and taking advantage of the coolness caused by the arrival of a bizarre cloud that was covering the sun, giving the whole valley a strange colour that made it look like honey poured on a large table.

Celeste had left her mother to look after the baby who was sleeping, and had gone for a walk in the village, with the specific purpose of going to thank the midwife. The main street was deserted, and even in the alleys that divided the houses, usually animated by women dedicated to embroidery and sewing, there was not a soul; it was very strange, because the only way to escape that oppressive heat was to seek refuge in the shade of the houses, where a little ventilation made work and conversation pleasant.

Liburna, the bitch they had rescued from the cold during that dreadful March snowfall, had followed them for a while, then she must have tired, because she had suddenly disappeared. She was a really good dog: she hardly ever barked, she ate only when she was given food without making too much fuss, and she had become very attached to Celeste, who showered her with attention and caresses.

As soon as she arrived in front of the midwife's house, she called out loudly, but got no answer; she pushed to open the door and found it was already open. She went in calling again, but the house was completely empty.

She decided to go back to her home: perhaps her baby had woken up and was demanding his feed.

Only then did she notice the cloud that had covered the sky, colouring the houses in the village and making them look like large mountains of honey.

Riccardo had gone into the woods, to thank God for the miraculous intervention of the previous day. He had not slept a wink that night, thinking about what to offer the Lord in gratitude; he had then decided that he would ask him directly.
"It will be a golden child," he had commented cheerfully after seeing his son in Celeste's arms, who had smiled smugly at him.
A son of his own. Now he really felt like a man. Edoardo had told him that a man cannot consider himself a man until he has guaranteed his descendants; he had then begun to cry, thinking back to the sad fate that befell his family.
At that moment, Riccardo had decided that if he ever had children, he would defend them at the cost of his own life against the snares of men and nature.
He was aware of everything that had happened. He had arrived home and found Celeste dead together with the baby; then he had returned to the stream and after running home again Celeste and the baby were fine. It was indeed a miracle. And he was the chosen one. Or perhaps his son Edoardo was, who knows. One thing was certain: God loved him. And he loved God. He thought back with dread to the horrible blasphemies he had shouted in front of the lifeless bodies of his loved ones, but he was sure that God had forgiven him.
As Riccardo waited seated on the usual stone, a great cloud covered the sun, and a river of honey descended from the sky, colouring the trees of the forest and all that belonged to that valley.

Chapter Ten

The circle is now closed. All the pieces are coming together. The time has come to sweep time away. Only space will exist, but soon that too will disappear. I will be alone.

And finally I will no longer be God. I will be ordinary again. Still this music!

1

Zimbaldi stopped the car in the forecourt of the farmhouse, raising a fuss that hung in mid-air for a few seconds.

"Where is the valley?" asked Smith as he got out of the car, imitated by the other three.

"It's there, beyond that pine forest," replied Roberto, pointing in the direction with his finger.

"Let's go." said Smith decisively, proceeding towards the pine forest with short but quick steps, so much so that Zimbaldi, Roberto and Elaine struggled not a little to keep up.

When they reached the beginning of the pine forest, Roberto showed the others the path through it; the journey was not very long, and they soon found themselves beyond the large trees.

They were astonished.

A large valley opened up before them, but it was not as deserted as when Roberto and Elaine had last seen it: there was a medieval village built two or three hundred metres away from the stream, and on the opposite side was a large forest.

The four of them looked at each other without a word; then Professor Smith walked slowly down the gently sloping path that led to the village, motioning to the others to follow him.

Zimbaldi hesitated, then followed the others reluctantly.

Francesco Zimbaldi was a coward; when he happened to unintentionally find a horror film on the tv, he would immediately change the channel, so as not to run the risk of spending the next few nights in the dark. Once he had wanted to be a hero: he had turned up at the local branch of Avis determined to become a blood donor.

They had made him sit on one of the comfortable chairs in the collection room, but as soon as the nurse had approached him with the syringe in her hand, he had fainted, immediately ending a brilliant future in the ranks of blood donors.

The next day, very angry with himself, he had registered with the organ donor section, hoping that after his death a part of his body might be of some use.

When Luca had heard this, his joking comment had been: 'They'll take your brain for sure. It's new, it's never been used!"

Suddenly a cloud darkened the sun, colouring everything amber, and the notes of Mozart's symphony in G minor spread through the air.

"What... what's going on?" asked Elaine, clinging to Roberto's arm.

"Nothing good, I suppose," Zimbaldi replied in a strange premonition.

"We are at the end. The mind that created all this somehow managed to stop time." noted Smith as he looked at the motionless cloud in front of the sun.

"But who is it?" asked Elaine again, "and what does it want from us?"

I don't know... though..." the sentence died on Smith's lips as Elaine's hysterical voice ripped through the silence.

"Professor, Roberto is gone! He's...he's gone!"

Smith looked at the void left by Roberto for a moment, then sighed, "I thought so. I didn't want to believe it, but this proves it."

"What does that mean?" asked Zimbaldi as Elaine slumped to the ground holding her face in her hands.

"That Roberto is the mastermind of all this. He is the one who created the village, Celeste, Riccardo. And also all of us and this music. I could tell by his hesitation this morning to accept what I had said. It was as if he was afraid to see that my supposition was correct. He wants to remain attached to this world, but something is trying to prevent it. Something independent of his will,' replied Smith, as Elaine looked at him, barely holding back tears.

"Why did he disappear?" asked Zimbaldi again.

"Maybe he has to decide. He has to fight, either with himself or with something I cannot identify. He has to decide whether to make this world live or destroy it. But it is not only up to him. Do you realise? He has given us a past, a life, he has given us form and substance: for us, he is truly God. Riccardo, in his simplicity, understood this before we did. Who knows why the Middle Ages, who knows why us Americans, who knows why everything. I have the impression that I am a memory of Roberto that has come to life, or something he always wanted and never got. The fact that Roberto experienced all this with us gives us hope... maybe it will even give us a future."

"Then we are just a figment of the imagination... we don't exist!" said Zimbaldi in a voice that betrayed a growing fear.

"And why not? What does it mean to exist? We exist, we breathe, we speak. We are alive, real... only we are in Roberto's world. In a different reality. If he wants he can destroy us, otherwise he lets us live. Which I fervently hope, although given my age, I don't have much time left now.' Smith replied, wandering his gaze into the valley.

"But who is Roberto really? God?" asked Zimbaldi, looking at Smith and envying his apparent calm.

"There are many things we ignore, and may never understand. I don't know who Roberto is. Yes, perhaps he is God. And he certainly is to us anyway. More I cannot say, because I don't have enough information."

"I...I love him." said Elaine with a thread in her voice, "I want to live together with Roberto. No matter what world. I couldn't be without him."

"That is my greatest hope. That for your sake he will make the right decision."

In that instant, the amber that coloured everything in that world became brighter and brighter, absorbing that universe in a vortex of blinding light; shapes and colours no longer existed, thoughts suddenly faded away. Everything was sucked out of the mind that had created it, and rested in two square centimetres of brain matter as big as the whole universe.

Chapter Eleven

1

Roberto opened his eyes.

He saw everything veiled, as if through an opaque glass.

He tried to move his head, but couldn't, so he looked left and right, to try to at least understand where he was.

He saw amber-coloured walls around him, and could distinctly hear Mozart's G minor symphony; he recognised it immediately, because he was a great fan of classical music.

His head ached as if a drill was piercing it; he felt something inside his nose, but he could not tell what it was.

An indistinct figure approached him, and he heard an excited voice speaking broken, nonsensical words.

"Maria... quickly... move your eyes!"

He couldn't understand...

My goodness, what happened? Did we have an accident with Zimbaldi's car?

Elaine! Where's Elaine?

His eyes began to work better, and the indistinct figure from just before turned out to be a nurse; next to her was another nurse, older, who was peering at him with interest.

'Can you hear me? Don't force yourself to speak... give me a nod with your eyes,' the woman said as she came within an inch of his face.

Roberto tried to speak, but could not even open his mouth. Then he blinked twice, and heard the nurse

say in a shrill, high pitched voice, 'He did it! Maria, did you see that? He did it!"
"I saw, I saw... let's go and get the doctor now," said the elderly nurse taking her by the arm and dragging her towards the door.
For some strange reason, Roberto's senses were heightened a hundredfold, and he could hear all the smallest noises; then, he distinctly heard the two women talking as they left the room.
"I don't know if it's a good thing that he woke up from his coma... assuming he actually woke up... and then after two years! How are we going to tell him?"
Maria nodded, "And that's not the worst thing. Do you think he's noticed his legs yet?"
"I don't think so. Anyway, we'll deal with the problems one at a time, as they arise. Let's go get the doctor right away. In the meantime, turn off the music."
The nurse turned off the stereo equipment and the two left.
Two years! Two years in a coma! But what year is this?
Suddenly something unlocked in Roberto's head, and his life appeared to him as a series of slides projected on a large screen passing rapidly inside his head.

His childhood spent in the constant terror of a strict father; the classical high school and then the decision to be a teacher; the happiness of his marriage and the relief after the divorce; his active involvement in a city district that re-enacted medieval spectacles; the trip to America, the best thing that had ever happened to him. The guitar, which had been for him the enthusiasm of his youth and a sweet companion in the years that followed; his great love for Tuscany, which reciprocated by offering him beautiful spectacles of art and nature; his wonder at the sea, an immense source of greatness and respect.

And finally love, the true love, always desired but never had.

In an instant he realised that all this had mixed with the amber with which the walls of that room were coloured and with the classical music he heard day after day.

He realised that he had managed to create an ideal world for himself, a world in which he was truly what he wanted to be in real life.

He looked at the room once more. It was just like the room in his world. There was also the screen, the window and the front door with the glass at the top.

Two years in a coma! What did that nurse say about my legs?

He felt them normal. He tried to move one of them, and it seemed to respond to his calls. He pulled himself together and managed to move an arm to feel them.

They were no longer there. He had lost both legs. They had probably been amputated as a result of the accident. He now remembered the car that had hit him and he also remembered the frightened face in the passenger compartment. It was a woman, and she had Elaine's face.

So he decided with all his might to do the only thing left to do.

Chapter Twelve

I am back. Now I will never leave. It's nice here...it's not hot, it's not cold...and everything is so veiled in amber. I only miss the music...but I'm sure it will start again soon. I am again God.

1

After a few minutes, the nurses and the doctor re-entered the room. The frantic ticking of the ventilating machine, which was allowing Roberto to breathe, warned them that something was wrong, and they saw to their dismay that the patient no longer had his oxygen tubes inserted into his nose.
They were clutched in his right hand, which was dangling outside the bed.
Roberto's eyes were closed, as if he were asleep. But he was no longer breathing.
The nurse rushed to the machine, pulled off the tubes connected to the cannula and inserted the mask, which she immediately forced onto the patient's face.
After a few moments that seemed eternal, Roberto's chest began to rise and fall rhythmically and the nurse breathed a sigh of relief.
The doctor glanced at the machine chart behind the bed and took Roberto's pulse; then he lifted his eyelids, directing a beam of light into his eyes with a small flashlight; then he shook his head and walked towards the door.

'I don't know if he was actually out of the coma before... the fact is that the interruption of oxygen to his brain lasted too long. He is in a coma again. To be on the safe side we'll do a CT scan in the afternoon, but I'm afraid he won't recover this time," he said turning to the nurse.
"Turn the music back on before you leave."

Chapter Thirteen

0

At the hour of sunset, anyone observing that beautiful honey-coloured valley would have been amazed to see a man and a woman running towards each other, embracing and losing themselves in a long, interminable, sweet kiss; turning their eyes towards the end of the valley, they would also have noticed two distinguished professors of medieval history smilingly enjoying the spectacle, thinking that this time love had conquered even death.

Valerio Di Piramo

Valerio Di Piramo was born and grew up in his native Tuscany. Lively and enterprising, from an early age he showed interest and curiosity in science, music and theatre, a passion that soon marked his artistic life. In addition to having composed around sixty pieces of music, he has written forty-five plays, performed by more than six hundred companies. He boasts about three hundred performances a year in Italy, and some comedies have been staged in Argentina, New Zealand, Canada, Australia, Russia and half of Europe. In Iran, the play "Wedding Gift" was published in Persian, under the title "The Tibetan Bell." The collaboration with Cristian Messina also resulted in the two plays "Leonardo e la magia del tempo" and "Sherlock Holmes e il mistero di Lady Margaret."

Translated by Linda June Lingham & Domen co Ippolito